The Joy of Not Working

The Joy of Not Working

A Book for the Retired, Unemployed, and Overworked

Ernie J. Zelinski

Ten Speed Press
Berkeley, California

This book is dedicated to you, the reader. I hope you will use the principles found in *The Joy of Not Working* to enhance your life as well as to better the world in which we live.

First published in Canada in 1991 by Visions International Publishing.
Published in Japanese by Kodansha Publishers, Tokyo, Japan; in Chinese by Yuan-Liou Publishing Co., Taipei, Taiwan; in Korean by Joong-Ang Daily News, Seoul, South Korea; and in Spanish by Ediciones Gestión 2000, S.A., Barcelona, Spain.

Ten Speed Press
P.O. Box 7123
Berkeley, CA 94707

Distributed in Australia by E.J. Dwyer Pty Ltd; in New Zealand by Tandem Press; in South Africa by Real Books; and in the United Kingdom and Europe by Airlift Books.

Cover design by Victor Ichioka
Interior design and typesetting by Jeff Brandenburg/ImageComp
Original illustrations by Vern Busby
Printed in Canada

Calvin and Hobbes by Bill Watterson, Mr. Boffo by Joe Martin, and Bizarro by Piraro used by permission of United Press Syndicate.

Library of Congress Cataloging-in-Publication Data on file with publisher.

1 2 3 4 5 — 01 00 99 98 97

Contents

Preface

This book is intended to make you a winner. After the first 50,000 copies of *The Joy of Not Working* sold, I updated and enlarged it to make it more relevant for the late 1990s and the start of the new millennium. I also included a few of the several hundred letters I received from people who read the original version.

Unlike most how-to books on winning, this book is not about winning at a job or making money. Nor is it a book about winning at competitive games. It is about winning when you aren't working, in a way that is not competitive, but still very rewarding.

> Everything has been figured out except how to live.
> —Jean-Paul Sartre

You're a winner when you have a zest for life, when you wake up every morning excited about the day. You're a winner when you enjoy what you're doing, and you're a winner when you pretty well know what you want to do with the rest of your life.

Whether you are retired, unemployed, or working, you can use *The Joy of Not Working* as a practical and reliable guide to creating a paradise away from the workplace. Because all of us need reminders from time to time about the obvious and the not-so-obvious, we can all use a handy guide on how to enhance our leisure time.

This book is the result of my education, an education which has nothing to do with the curricula in place at schools and universities. I acquired this education through my personal experiences, far removed from my formal education.

At the age of twenty-nine, I embarked on a new career. Having lost my job, I decided that I wanted to be a creative loafer for a year or so. Although my new career was supposed to be temporary, I have yet to return to a regular job.

In my last regular job, I allowed myself to be imprisoned by a system which isn't designed for free spirits. For almost six years, I worked for a government-owned utility, where I was supposed to work from nine to five. The nine-to-five job was more often an eight-to-six job with weekend work, mostly without extra compensation.

Having skipped vacations for over three years, I decided to take ten weeks off work one summer. Aside from the fact that I did not have approval from my superiors, I thought this was a great idea. I really enjoyed those ten weeks. Despite the idea's brilliance, I ended up being fired from my job as a professional engineer. The verdict was that I had violated company policy by taking the extended vacation.

Obviously, my superiors didn't like what I had done. Despite my high performance evaluations and my lengthy period without a vacation, the company terminated my employment when I returned to work. I am not sure if my termination was solely due to my violating company policy. Perhaps my superiors were envious of how much I enjoyed myself during my extended vacation. Many supervisors, especially those in government, don't like dealing with subordinates who are enjoying themselves.

For the first few weeks, I was bitter about being fired. Having been a dedicated and productive worker, I knew I had made many important contributions to this company. Undoubtedly, a great injustice had been done when they fired me, a valuable employee.

> What's the use of being a genius if you can't use it as an excuse for being unemployed?
>
> —Gerald Barzan

A big turning point for me was the day when I realized my firing was a blessing in disguise. Along with reluctantly admitting I wasn't indispensable, I also lost interest in a regular nine-to-five job. I decided, from then on, to make sure that I took as much time off as I could, especially in summers. A normal job was now out of the question; my career as a professional engineer was over.

For the next two years, I didn't work at all, nor did I attend any educational institution. My purpose in life was to be happy without a job. I ended up missing my former engineering job about as much as I missed the old LP record by the Ventures that I lost about fifteen years ago—not much.

What did I do during this time? Although at times I had very little money, I lived what I consider to be a very prosperous life. I engaged in constructive and satisfying activities too numerous to mention. The main point is that I celebrated life. I grew as a person and went through a transformation of my values. During those two years, I truly earned my Doctorate in Leisure (which no university has as yet granted me).

After two years of total leisure, I decided never to work in any month without an "r" in it. To me, May, June, July, and August are suited

Mr. Zelinski, Harvard University, always thankful for all major contributions to society, today would like to grant you the honorary degree of Doctor of Leisure.

mainly for leisure activities. In fact, because I enjoy my free time so much, I have successfully avoided having a regular nine-to-five job for over a decade. For all intents and purposes, I have been in temporary retirement or semi-retirement since I was in my late twenties.

Over the years, many people have asked me how I am able to utilize so much leisure time without getting bored. After talking to these people, I realized many individuals have problems attaining satisfaction from their spare time. One day, it also occurred to me that there has been very little written on how to manage leisure time. That is when the idea for this book was conceived. Since I believe anyone can fill their spare time with constructive and exciting activities, I decided a book on how to enjoy leisure time would help many people.

Leisure is the most challenging responsibility a man can be offered.
—William Russell

Throughout this book, I share my thoughts about leisure and a number of my experiences. To give a much broader perspective to leisure, I don't draw from only my own experiences. The greater part of this

book is the result of studying and listening to the stories, experiences, and aspirations of other people.

This book isn't a highly academic one. I avoid great detail and academic jargon, which most readers wouldn't enjoy. Instead, I made the book as short as possible, so the message is presented with the fewest possible words. The book's format includes text, exercises, cartoons, diagrams, and quotations, to appeal to the many learning styles that individuals have. This format was used in my first book, *The Joy of Not Knowing It All* (originally published under the title *The Art of Seeing Double or Better in Business*). The many positive comments that I received from readers convinced me this format works best in getting my message across in an interesting and entertaining way.

"The Life of Riley" has been a popular expression for decades. A person living the Life of Riley is able to live comfortably without working. This book is about how you can live the Life of Riley; however, what it takes to live the Life of Riley may surprise you.

Success is a matter of luck—just ask any failure.
—Unknown Wise Person

Success at leisure isn't based on being lucky in life. It takes the effort to follow and apply certain principles, the basis for this book. By following these principles, you will be able to discover and choose some new directions in your life. You will be on the road to many wonderful and fulfilling experiences, which you could never experience at any job. You will be able to claim, as I am able, that you can be much happier away from the workplace than in it.

If you want to add to the variety, tone, and quality of your life, this book will be a valuable asset. I trust *The Joy of Not Working* will entertain, challenge, influence, and motivate you to attain an exciting and rewarding life of leisure.

—Ernie J. Zelinski

CHAPTER 1

You Too Can Live the Life of Riley

A Grand Time to Loaf

On the second day that he was visiting a large city, a wealthy and somewhat eccentric traveler encountered six panhandlers who he had seen soliciting money the previous day. The panhandlers were now all lying in the sun, obviously taking a break from the duties related to their chosen profession. The panhandlers looked up as the traveler approached.

The traveler decided to have some fun. He offered a $1000 bill to the panhandler who could prove that he was the laziest. Hoping to claim the prize, five of the panhandlers jumped up to take part in the contest. Each one proceeded to demonstrate in varying ways, such as by sitting down while soliciting money from tourists, how much lazier than his colleagues he could be at his panhandling.

> I am a friend of the workingman, and I would rather be his friend, than be one.
>
> —Clarence Darrow

After an hour, having watched the five competitors with amusement, the traveler made his decision and awarded the $1000 bill. He concluded that the sixth panhandler, who had refrained from the competition, was definitely the laziest. The sixth panhandler had remained lying on the grass, reading a paper and enjoying the sun.

There is a moral to this story: Not working, when it is more appropriate to enjoy yourself loafing, can have its benefits.

This book is about the many pleasures to be enjoyed away from the workplace. It is about how you can, if retired, manage and enhance your large amount of spare time; if presently unemployed, enjoy your extra spare time while between jobs; or, if employed, better enjoy your limited spare time.

In other words, no matter what your situation, this book is about how you can get more satisfaction and pleasure from your leisure. Welcome to the joy of not working.

Leisure: The Opposite of Work, but Not Quite

"How do you define leisure?" This is an interesting question, but one that is difficult to answer. A participant in a leisure-planning seminar I presented at a Canadian Association of Pre-retirement Planners conference posed this question to me.

Without a definite answer, I decided to follow one of my many principles of creativity—give the problem away. I asked the other seminar participants to define leisure.

After a great deal of discussion, we arrived at what appeared to be a consensus. We ended up defining leisure as "spare time over and above the time required to perform the necessities in life." This was good enough for us to continue.

Of course, this definition can lead to another good question: "What do you define as necessities in life?" Eating may be a necessity, but casual dining for an hour or two at a bistro is a pleasure. Casual dining is one of my favorite leisure activities. To others, eating is a necessity, and a bothersome activity.

Later, I looked up the definition of leisure in several dictionaries. Dictionaries commonly define leisure in such terms as "time free from required work, in which a person may rest, amuse oneself, and do the things one likes to do."

So where does eating fit into the dictionary definition? Is eating work? Is eating leisure? Or is eating something altogether different?

I wasn't about to take the time to locate the people responsible for the dictionary definition to see if they could clarify this confusion. I suspect they would have great difficulty in doing this for me.

> **DICTIONARY**
>
> **lei-sure** (le'zher or lezh'er), n.
> 1. the opposite of work but not quite. 2. somewhat of a paradox. 3. what a person does living the life of Riley.—adj. and adv. **lei'sure-ly.**
>
> **lem-on** (lem'un) n. 1. a small tropical fruit with pale yellow skin and very acid juice; 2. the tree, related to the orange, which bears this fruit; 3. a pale yellow color.—adj.
>
> **lem-on-ade** (lem'un-ād) n. a drink of sweetened water flavored with lemon juice.

After thinking about this question for some time, I was still a little puzzled. How can I define leisure to prevent the potential for endless questioning in my seminars? I just want to present my ideas on how to enjoy leisure. I don't want to be a philosopher, determining whether eating is leisure or leisure is eating.

I hate definitions.
—Benjamin Disraeli

Then I decided that the purpose for my seminars (and this book) is not to establish a universal and perfect definition for leisure. Leisure will always mean different things to different people. However, loosely defined, leisure is the time an individual spends away from work to do the things he or she wants to do.

It is up to you and me to define work and leisure for our personal needs. Subsequently, it is up to you and me to find out what we, as individuals, want to do in our spare time. Of course, we also have to actually do what we want.

Actually doing what we say we would enjoy is easier said than done. There is an interesting paradox here: Leisure is about not working; however, in order to attain satisfaction from our leisure, we will have to "work" at it. As odd as it may seem, leisure is the opposite of work, but it is still something that may require a great deal of effort.

The Illusions of Leisure, Retirement, and Lotteries

By choice or by chance, all of us, sooner or later, have to deal with how to utilize and enjoy leisure time. There is no doubt that what we do with our spare time will determine the quality of our lives.

Because it was once a rather rare commodity, leisure was considered a luxury for many centuries. Only recently has leisure become abundant enough for some people to expect decades of it through lengthy retirement.

Leisure time in great measure is the ultimate goal of many North Americans. Everyone desires at least a certain amount. Some people claim their goal is to have nothing but leisure on their hands, so they can live the Life of Riley. Yet, many people aren't prepared for handling substantial leisure time. Sustained leisure has become a burden to many, even though they are healthy and in a favorable financial position to enjoy many activities.

Most of us reserve the enjoyment of leisure for the future; often the future arrives too soon. We end up with much more spare time than we are accustomed to when we retire or are laid off. The reality, then, is we have large amounts of time to spend on leisure activities. Reality is often quite sobering. Whether we have found our jobs exciting and stimulating or boring and depressing, many of us are in for a big surprise when confronted with an increase in spare time.

It is paradoxical but nonetheless true that the nearer man comes to his goal to make his life easy and abundant, the more he undermines the foundations of a meaningful existence.
—Franz Alexander

Leisure without problems is one of life's illusions. Once we experience an increase in our spare time, many of us are faced with new problems to replace the old. Various studies confirm that many people have difficulty in handling spare time. One study by the United States Department of Commerce reported that only 58 percent of people were experiencing "a great deal" of satisfaction from how they spend their leisure time. This means that 42 percent of individuals could use substantial help in enhancing the quality in their

leisure. Even some of the people who are getting a great deal of satisfaction may not be experiencing as much satisfaction as they would like. Many of these people probably could use some help as well.

The majority of us will spend the greater part of our adult lives working. Taking into account getting ready for work, commuting to work, talking about our jobs, and worrying about getting laid off, we will have spent more time during our working lives thinking about work than thinking about all our other concerns in life.

Associated with thinking about work is thinking about how great it will be when we don't have to work anymore. Many of us dream about how much better things will be when we have much more leisure time.

When I worked as an engineer, I was amazed (and dejected) to hear young engineers and technicians in their twenties spending a lot of time talking about pensions and retirement. Quite frankly, in my twenties I had many more interesting subjects to talk about. (If you are interested in what they were, buy me dinner, and we'll have a most interesting conversation.)

Society leads us to believe that retirement and happiness are one and the same. Retirement is supposed to be the great escape from the stresses inherent in most jobs. It is supposed to mean a fulfilling life derived from many enjoyable and rewarding activities.

Oh to reach the point of death and realize one has not lived at all.
—Henry David Thoreau

Up until a few years ago, I, like most people in my generation, allowed myself to be influenced by society's programming. I believed that increased leisure was something everyone looked forward to and enjoyed once they retired. Since then, I have learned it is dangerous, more often than not, to accept the teachings and the ideas most people in society adopt. The masses are frequently wrong. Certain factions in society regularly sell us a false bill of goods. We are not given the complete picture; the finer things in life often turn out to be different from what society has led us to believe they would be.

Being unable to retire can be a tragedy, as can the actual act of retiring. Many individuals nearing retirement have fears about imminent diminished purpose and activity. Once they retire, the results can be negative, even tragic. Death or senility is common within two years of retirement; suicide is also a possibility. In fact, the suicide rate for American men is four times higher in retirement than in any other stage in life.

In this world there are only two tragedies. One is not getting what one wants, and the other is getting it.
—Oscar Wilde

Winning a major lottery in North America is supposed to be an event that enhances our lives to immeasurable levels. Becoming a millionaire should give us the life about which we have always dreamed. Not all the evidence supports this notion. A winner of a major lottery in New York expressed regret after having quit his job. "I really miss that truck driving. The biggest loss of my life is not having someone to tell me what to do." These were the words of a millionaire ex-trucker, as reported in the book *Suddenly Rich*. The book's authors, Jerry LeBlanc and Rena Dictor LeBlanc, studied wealthy people who had acquired sudden fortunes.

The LeBlancs found certain people with unlimited leisure time on their hands weren't very happy. After having been given a mandatory routine by employers for so long, these people had trouble dealing with days totally lacking in structure and purpose. Many other lottery winners continued to work, despite being harassed by co-workers and friends about working at a job they didn't need for financial purposes.

A study by Challenger, Gray & Christmas, Inc., found that over 50 percent of people accepting early retirement packages were more than happy to return to work after three months in retirement. Retirement was not what many people thought it would be. A life comprising total leisure wasn't all that enjoyable. With all work's negatives, it wasn't so bad after all.

Guess I'll apply for work again. After having been retired for six months, I am really looking forward to returning to the misery of

Two Sides to Taking It Easy

For many people, taking it easy is difficult to handle. Perhaps, living the life of Riley wasn't easy even for Riley. To the unprepared, having a great deal of spare time can bring on many anxieties.

You may have the same difficulties if you don't develop your ability to enjoy many leisure activities. If you haven't developed a love for leisure by the time you retire, you may feel the Life of Riley is the biggest rip-off since the last time you bought the Brooklyn Bridge.

Here are some common problems that people have with their leisure time:

- ➤ Boredom with oneself and others
- ➤ No real satisfaction from leisure activities
- ➤ All dressed up and nowhere to go
- ➤ All dressed up, somewhere to go, but no one to go with
- ➤ Friction with spouse when time together increases
- ➤ Not enough things to do
- ➤ So much to do and no time to do it
- ➤ Hard time deciding what to do
- ➤ Bankroll of a peasant but tastes of a millionaire
- ➤ Bankroll of a millionaire but poverty consciousness of a peasant

➤ Feeling guilty about having fun and enjoying oneself
➤ Enjoyment only from things that are illegal, immoral, or unhealthy

The other side of leisure is much more positive. Unlimited spare time can be a great opportunity in life. Many people are able to adjust to a life of total leisure without missing a stride. To some, the leisurely life is even more satisfying than they expected. They have become more active than ever before; each day is a new adventure. These people will claim nothing can be as enjoyable as a leisurely lifestyle.

If a man could have just half of his wishes, he would double his troubles.
—Benjamin Franklin

When you are able to enjoy leisure time to the fullest, your life will be enhanced to immeasurable levels. Success at handling leisure will contribute to a life that many on this earth can only dream about. Some benefits available to you from an increase in your leisure time are:

➤ A higher quality of life
➤ Personal growth
➤ Improved health
➤ Higher self-esteem
➤ Less stress and a more relaxed lifestyle
➤ Satisfaction from challenging activities
➤ Excitement and adventure
➤ A more balanced lifestyle if employed
➤ A sense of self-worth, even if unemployed
➤ Quality of family life increases

The difference between success and failure at anything is often slim. Having covered the problems and benefits of leisure, let's look at what is essential for receiving as many benefits as possible from leisure time.

The difference between success and failure at anything is often slim.

The following exercise is just one of several you will encounter in the book. You will get a lot more from this book if you take the time to attempt all the exercises. You can add to the answers, where a choice of answers is given, if none of the others are suitable to you.

Exercise 1-1. The Essentials

Which of the factors below are essential for attaining success at managing and enjoying leisure time?

- ➤ Excellent health
- ➤ Living in an exciting city
- ➤ Having many friends from different walks of life
- ➤ A charming personality
- ➤ Owning a motor home
- ➤ A love for travel
- ➤ Athletic ability
- ➤ Good looks
- ➤ Excellent physical condition
- ➤ Financial independence
- ➤ A beach cabin
- ➤ Living in a warm climate
- ➤ Having had good parents
- ➤ A great marriage or relationship
- ➤ Having many hobbies

Before we discuss what is essential, let's look at two individuals who are having trouble with leisure, and one person who isn't. This gives us a better indication of what is essential for attaining satisfaction in leisure.

The Life of Riley Can Be Elusive

Recently, I talked to Delton, who is sixty-seven years old, financially secure, and plays tennis (sometimes better than me) at the club where I play. Although Delton liked the company he worked with for many years, he didn't like its policy on mandatory retirement at sixty-five.

When he first retired, Delton had no idea what he should do with his time. He was lost. Delton, two years into retirement, is now happy his company allows him to work part-time. His time away from the job is not well spent (except when he whips me in a game of tennis). Delton even confided in me that he hasn't liked weekends for a long time. He has always had a hard time deciding what to do on his days off.

Rich, another member at my tennis club, is another example of someone who had problems with his spare time. The difference between Delton and Rich is that Rich yearned to retire early. Like many people in the city in which I live, Rich fantasized about moving to the West Coast to live the Life of Riley. Rich had his wish come true when he was only forty-four. Having worked with a police force since he was nineteen, Rich was able to retire with a decent pension after working only twenty-five years.

People waste more time waiting for someone to take charge of their lives than they do in any other pursuit.
—*Gloria Steinem*

After Rich moved away to the West Coast to enjoy the Life of Riley, he realized that he didn't have too much in common with Riley. Rich found handling unlimited spare time extremely difficult. He responded by opening a business. When he lost his shirt on that venture (not serious—you don't need a shirt in West Coast weather), he tried several other things, including going back to work for a short time. Rich is still undecided on how he can best deal with retirement. This is somewhat unfortunate, considering Rich is in an enviable position to which many people aspire.

Unemployed Stockbroker Lives Life of Riley

In 1987, North American newspapers reported on the plight of stockbrokers, who were having it tough after the October 19, 1987 market crash. Young executives, who had known a bull market and the expensive lifestyles it brought, were bewildered and astounded. Many, who were about to lose their $200,000 to $500,000-a-year jobs, were saying they couldn't take other jobs at $100,000 a year because their personal expenses were too high. (I'm sure these stories brought tears to many readers' eyes, as they did to mine.)

The only thing some people do is grow older.
—*Ed Howe*

Of course, it was unthinkable for these stockbrokers to consider unemployment for a few months, or even a year. Due to their expensive lifestyles, these executives couldn't comprehend the alternative of temporarily being without a job and income.

My friend Denny was a stockbroker during the period before the crash. He hadn't been a top producer and had saved very little money. After the crash, Denny left the business altogether. He didn't immediately go looking for another job (not even a low paying one at $100,000 a year). Although Denny had very little money to live the Life of Riley, he decided to take it easy for at least a year so he could enjoy a different lifestyle.

During the time Denny was unemployed, he became as content as anyone could be in this world. He was relaxed, he had a smile he couldn't lose, and he was a treat to be around because of his positive nature. I knew many working people who were making good incomes at their high-status jobs, but I didn't know one working person who was as happy as Denny. He took the better part of a year to live the Life of Riley.

With an evening coat and a white tie, anybody, even a stockbroker, can gain a reputation for being civilized.
—Oscar Wilde

Denny has since returned to the workforce in another city. On a visit back to my home city, Denny mentioned that, although he was enjoying his new career, he was yearning for the time when he again could take a year or two off just to enjoy life. There is no doubt in my mind that Denny, unlike Rich and Delton, will enjoy the Life of Riley when he permanently retires.

Riley's Secret

No matter what your age, sex, occupation, and income, you can experience the many joys of not working. I can say this simply because I personally have been able to be as happy, if not happier, not working as I was working. If I can do it, so can you. My firsthand experience at spending over half of my adult years without a job has given me insight into what it takes to be a success away from the job. My success has been the result of paying attention to the things I must do to be happy at leisure and being committed to doing them.

I haven't been blessed with any special talents and abilities that you don't have. Other people, like Denny, who experience great enjoyment in their spare time, are also quite normal. Success in life's adventures isn't the result of having some huge advantage over others. We all have the ability required to make life a success; the key is to acknowledge our own talents and put them to good use.

What then are the differences between people who are able to live the Life of Riley and those who aren't? Why is my friend Denny so content with having nothing but free time on his hands, while my two acquaintances, Delton and Rich, find unlimited free time a burden?

Let's return to Exercise 1-1 on page 8. If you chose any item that was on the list, you are a victim of your own incorrect thinking about what it takes to master leisure. Not one item that I listed is essential for successfully living the Life of Riley. Every item on the list may be an asset, but none is essential. I want to stress that we can discount financial

independence as an essential item. Delton and Rich are much better off financially than Denny was. If financial independence is essential, Delton and Rich should be happy in their leisure and Denny unhappy in his, instead of the other way around. In Chapter 11, we will look at the role money plays in the enjoyment of leisure. Some people will argue that excellent health is essential. Health is an important asset, but many people who have health problems are still able to enjoy leisure and life in general.

Then what is essential? The Life of Riley is nothing more than a state of mind. Denny has the one essential ingredient—a healthy attitude. Riley himself had to have a healthy attitude to live the good life. Synchronicity must have struck, because I received the following letter from Dick Phillips of Portsmouth, Hampshire, England, while I was in the middle of updating the first three chapters of this book.

> *They are able because they think they are able.*
>
> —*Virgil*

Dear Ernie,

My wife Sandy and I were on an Air Canada flight to Vancouver this summer to commence a "Life of Riley" retirement holiday in your lovely country when a fellow female passenger introduced me to your book *The Joy of Not Working*.

I later obtained a copy at Duthie's Bookstore and read it when I returned home. (Riley did not allow time for reading on holidays.) I am fifty-four years of age and have worked since I was fifteen years old: first, as a fitter and turner apprentice, then as a seagoing-ships engineer before joining the County Police for a thirty-year career. Your book gives much sound advice, some I have been following for years. I have enjoyed developing interests outside work while still working. When I retired last November, I enjoyed the freedom to parcel up my time and develop interests that include hiking, cycling, old car restoration, model engineering, painting and DIY projects. You are right a positive attitude to life in retirement is essential.

In your book, you write about a fellow officer named Rich who, like me, retired in an enviable position but found life difficult. I hope he has now read your book, and he is developing that inner self that makes all things possible. Meanwhile, I am looking forward to next year, when I join a team building a large, wooden sailing ship for disabled people, and later finding time to revisit Canada.

Regards to Riley,

Dick Phillips

Note that Dick Phillips, like Denny, has a healthy attitude about leisure, an important attribute for enjoying life. Nothing can replace a healthy attitude, for success in life. If you don't have a healthy attitude, then you must put in the effort and develop one. This book is mainly about developing and maintaining such an attitude about life and leisure.

CHAPTER 2

What You See Is What You Get

Thinking for a Change

We can change the quality of our lives by changing the context in which we view our circumstances. Two people can be faced with the same situation, such as being fired from a job, yet one will view it as a blessing, and the other will view it as a curse. Changing the context of the situation depends on our ability to challenge our attitudes and be flexible in our thinking.

Most of us don't take the time to reflect upon what we are thinking or why we think what we do. To affect a change in our thinking, we must start thinking for a change. By challenging our thinking, we set the stage for fresh perspectives and new values to replace outmoded beliefs. Challenging the way we think about work and its benefits helps us develop a healthy attitude about leisure. Never challenging the way we think has at least two inherent dangers:

> *Most people think only once or twice a year. I have made myself an international reputation by thinking once or twice a week.*
> *—George Bernard Shaw*

> ➤ We may get locked into one way of thinking, without seeing other alternatives that may be more appropriate.

> We may adopt a set of values that, at the time, makes a lot of sense. Time will pass; with time, things will change. The original values will no longer be appropriate, but we will still continue to function with the original, outmoded values.

Old Dogs Can Learn New Tricks

Draw a black dot like the one above on a white board and ask a class of adult students what they see. Practically everyone will say they see a black dot and only a black dot. Place a similar dot in front of a class of children in grade school, and the answers will excite you. You will hear fascinating answers like:

> darkness outside a round window
> a black bear rolled up in a ball
> a hubcap
> a horse's eye

> a black marble
> the inside of a pipe
> a chocolate cookie

We all come into this world blessed with great imaginations. As children, we all have the capacity and flexibility to see the world from many different points of view. Because, as children, we pay attention to practically everything around us, our ability to enjoy life is remarkable.

Grown-ups never understand anything by themselves, and it is tiresome for children to be always and forever explaining things to them.

—From The Little Prince by Antoine de Saint-Exupéry

At some point in childhood, most of us start to lose these abilities. Society, educational institutions, and our parents influence us by telling us what we should expect. We are conditioned to look for acceptance. To be accepted socially, we stop questioning. We lose our mental flexibility, and we stop paying attention.

As a result our thinking becomes very structured. Our reluctance to change our beliefs and values fosters erroneous, incomplete, or outdated perceptions of the world. These distorted perceptions interfere with our creativity and our enjoyment of life.

Being creative goes hand in hand with having a healthy attitude. In any field of endeavor, creative people are the ones who are most successful over the long term. They see opportunity where others see insurmountable problems.

Researchers have found that the major difference between creative and uncreative people is that creative people simply think they are creative. The uncreative have become too structured and routine in their thinking and erroneously don't think of themselves as having what it takes to be creative.

Imperative to having a healthy attitude is realizing

What's the matter, Mitch? Did you lose all of your creativity when you turned fifty-five? Use what I use to get out of these situations!

that we have to continually challenge our perceptions to avoid inhabiting a world of delusions. People who don't develop a habit of carefully examining their own premises and beliefs run the risk of seeing a world that has little relationship to reality. The results of this destructive practice can be serious, ranging from disappointments to depression to mental illness.

Many people are uncomfortable with the notion that their own attitudes and beliefs are all that stop them from achieving success. Most frightening to them is having to give up their excuses for not winning at the game of life. My observation is that people who most resist change and the notion that their perceptions may be wrong most need to start thinking creatively to get their lives back on track to fulfillment.

Old dogs can learn new tricks, if they want to learn them. The only thing that will stop any one of us from learning new behaviors is ourselves. Age is commonly used as an

The dog too old to learn new tricks always has been.
—Unknown Wise Person

excuse. The age-old excuse of age has always been used by people who become structured in their thinking at an early age.

In other words, their attitudes toward and resistance to change—not their chronological age—have interfered with their ability to change. Adults who are open-minded and use their imaginations aren't hindered by age, when it comes to developing new values and behaviors.

In the Land of the Blind, One Eye Is King

Exercise 2-1. The Three Secrets to Fulfillment

A successful, but unhappy American entrepreneur had acquired a lot of wealth. He decided to retire and take it easy; however, he soon realized he was still not very happy.

Because his life was so empty, the entrepreneur decided to go in search of a Zen master who knew three important secrets for living life to the fullest. After twenty months of searching, the entrepreneur finally found this Zen master on top of an obscure high mountain.

The Zen master was happy to reveal the three secrets to having a happy and satisfying life. The entrepreneur was surprised by what he was told.

What were the three secrets?

1. _____
2. _____
3. _____

You're telling me, "Life is a joke!" Is that all there is to enlightenment?

One of the keys to enjoying the world more is to practice the habit of flexibility. There is an old French proverb: "In the land of the blind, one eye is king." Being flexible will allow you to see things in this world that others don't see.

For the above exercise, were you able to come up with the three secrets to fulfillment in life? According to the Zen master they are:

1. pay attention

2. pay attention

3. pay attention

Creative people pay attention to the world around them and see a lot of opportunity in life. Uncreative people, due to their inability to pay attention, erroneously perceive a lack of opportunity in their lives.

If you want a fulfilling life, learn to truly pay attention. The way to develop a healthy attitude is to develop your ability to focus your attention and consciousness on new things. You should also develop fresh ways of perceiving familiar things. If you are a rigid person, you will require effort, along with courage, to change your perceptions, and start experiencing life and leisure in new ways.

Only the most foolish of mice would hide in a cat's ear. But only the wisest of cats would think to look there.
—Scott Love

Without giving it much thought, some people will say that the management and enjoyment of leisure time is nothing more than common sense. I couldn't agree with this point of view more. But why do I have to write a book based on a lot of common sense? Because many people will go to extremes to complicate their lives when following the basics will do. In other words, common sense is not very common.

Are You Paying Attention?

All of us, to some degree, are not paying attention. We allow our perceptions to be affected by our judgments. Therefore, we don't see all there is to see.

Attempt the four exercises on the following two pages to test your ability to pay attention. See if you have the presence of mind to notice everything there is to see. Allow yourself a few minutes for doing all the exercises.

The obscure we see eventually. The completely obvious, it seems, take longer.
—Edward R. Murrow

Exercise 2-2. Looking at Perception

Look at the following two figures and then continue with the other exercises.

Figure 1

A bird
in the
the hand

is worth
two in
the ditch

Figure 2

Exercise 2-3. Triangles Galore

The diagram below is a perspective builder. You simply have to count the number of triangles in the diagram.

Exercise 2-4. Playing With Matches

The equation below is made from matchsticks. Each line in a character is one matchstick. This equation is wrong. Move just one matchstick to make the equation correct.

$$VI + II = VI$$

Exercise 2-5. Cycle Designed by a Psycho?

Although my undergraduate degree is in electrical engineering, a while ago I decided to design something mechanical. This is a design for a new tandem bicycle that I created to help people enjoy leisure. (I know you are impressed.) Analyze the merits of this design for a new tandem bicycle.

Perception Is Everything

If you noticed everything that there was to see in Figure 1 of Exercise 2-2, you should have read the following in the two boxes.

A bird in **the the** hand is worth two in the ditch.

Not seeing the two "the's" indicates that you are not seeing all there is to see. You also may be overlooking many solutions when solving your problems in life.

In Figure 2, you probably noticed a triangle that is whiter than the rest of the page. First, note that there is no actual triangle drawn there. Your eyes just imagined one being there. In addition, the whiteness of this mirage triangle is no brighter than the rest of the page. Just as you saw a triangle and brightness that weren't in this figure, you may be imagining many barriers or obstacles to solving your problems in life that aren't there.

In the figure in Exercise 2-3, most people see fewer than twenty-five triangles. Did you notice all there is to see? There are actually thirty-five different triangles in this figure. In Exercise 2-4, you may have generated a solution or two. If you did, that's great. However, if you stopped after only one or two solutions, that's not so great. I have over twenty solutions to this exercise, which you can get by taking the time to generate them yourself (or by paying a fortune to attend one of my seminars). If you generate only one solution to your problems at work or play, you are missing out on the opportunity to generate more exciting and effective solutions.

What do you think about my bicycle in Exercise 2-5? If your evaluation was all negative, you have not fully explored my design. Unless you put down some positive points and some negative ones, you have jumped to conclusions—without due consideration—about my "unusual" design. Your voice of judgment has stepped in too soon. You should have considered positive elements; such as, the rear wheel can be used as a spare in case the front tire goes flat. How about a more comfortable ride due to the two back wheels? This bicycle could also have an advantage over conventional ones for carrying heavy loads; it will be great for overweight people. People may want to buy it as a status symbol because it is a new and different design. There are many positive and negative elements in this design. To fully explore the merits of this design, you should consider all the advantages and disadvantages. Similarly, when evaluating your ideas or someone's suggestions, you should consider all of the advantages and disadvantages before making a decision.

Some men see things as they are and ask, "Why?" I see them as they have never been and ask, "Why not?"
—George Bernard Shaw

In life, perception is everything; what you see is what you get. You can be the judge of how well you paid attention in the previous exercises. If you didn't see all there was to see, you may want to start paying more attention to the world around you.

Only the Foolish and the Dead Don't Change

Today's world is changing at an unprecedented pace. To deal effectively with this change, you must ensure that your opinions, beliefs, and values aren't carved in stone. Avoid being a rigid person, and your life will be a lot easier in today's rapidly changing world.

Some people are afraid to change in any way because they feel that changing their values, beliefs, or opinions is a sign of weakness. On the contrary, the ability to change represents strength and a willingness to grow. There is much to be said for the saying that only the foolish and the dead never change their beliefs and opinions. As I implied before, no matter who you are, you can change.

I want to stress that the more inflexible you are, the more problems you will have in living and adjusting to our rapidly changing

To him, this bicycle represents leisure. To me, it represents work.

world. My experience in teaching creativity seminars reveals that people who most need to change their thinking are most resistant to change. The opposite is true with highly adaptive and creative people. To them, change is exciting. They are always willing to challenge their points of view, and they are willing to change them when change is necessary.

Looking past your present beliefs and perceptions may open up many new dimensions of life. Develop the presence of mind to question everything you believe. Learn to weed out old, unworkable beliefs. At the same time, learn to adopt new values and fresh behaviors to see whether they are workable.

Rediscover Your Creativity

Business Week magazine reported that a forty-year-old is about 2 percent as creative as a child of five. Obviously, we must encounter many blocks to expressing our imagination if we have lost over 90 percent of our creativity by the time we are forty. What happens to us?

The biggest block to our creativity is ourselves—when we allow ourselves to be influenced by social, organizational, and educational forces that urge conformity on us. We also erect many private barriers that rob us of the opportunity to use our imaginations. Fear of failure is one of the more effective robbers of our creativity, as are laziness and faulty perception. Despite these barriers, however, everyone is born with creative abilities, and everyone can rediscover these abilities.

Seventeen Principles of Creativity

To rediscover your creativity, just start using the following seventeen principles of creativity, which form the basis of my book, *The Joy of Not Knowing It All*. When you start applying these creativity principles to your work and play, your life will change immensely regardless of your occupation or age.

- Choose to be creative.
- Look for many solutions.
- Write your ideas down.
- Fully analyze your ideas.
- Define your goal(s).
- See problems as opportunities.
- Look for the obvious.
- Take risks.
- Dare to be different.
- Be unreasonable.
- Have fun and be foolish.
- Be spontaneous.
- Be in the now.
- Practice divergent thinking.
- Challenge rules and assumptions.
- Delay your decision.
- Be persistent.

Whether you want to be more creative at writing, painting, dancing, finding a new route home, or meeting a new person, you don't require special talent. What is necessary is your willingness to be imaginative.

Flat-Earth Thinkers on a Round World

Your ability to enjoy the wonderful world of leisure will be determined by how much you have been able to avoid being brainwashed by mainstream society. All societies try to impose morals and values on their members. As we see from history, these morals and values are often detrimental to many individuals and to society in general.

Faced with having to change our views or prove that there is no need to do so, most of us immediately get busy on the proof.
—John Kenneth Galbraith

Note that I am saying society *tries* to do this; society doesn't succeed with everyone. Not all members subscribe to the prevalent values and morals of their society. There are some people who pay attention. Individuals with presence of mind will not be influenced by society's wishes, if they see what society believes as suspect. These are the people who lay the groundwork for society to progressively change for the better.

Several centuries ago, despite evidence to the contrary, most people in the mainstream of society believed the earth was flat. This idea was not easily surrendered.

Holding on to outmoded beliefs is as common today as it was several centuries ago. People don't want to give up their long-held beliefs. They hate to admit their beliefs were wrong; this would be a blow to their egos. Belief becomes an incurable disease. Rather than subscribe to a new and different viewpoint that may be beneficial to them, people hang on to the old.

The fact that an opinion has been widely held is no evidence whatever that it is not entirely absurd; indeed in view of the silliness of the majority of mankind, a widespread belief is more likely to be foolish than sensible.
—Bertrand Russell

North American society, like most societies before it, thinks it is as progressive as it can be. Our society, however, is no different from many societies before it; it is infiltrated by many flat-earth thinkers. When it comes to work and leisure, many of our society's values and morals are outdated. Future societies may look at today's common beliefs about work and leisure as primitive, much as we look at the old belief that the world was flat as primitive.

CHAPTER 3

The Morality of Work Is the Morality of Slaves

Thinking About Work

If you want to enhance the quality of your life of leisure, challenging your own thinking about work is a good place to start. As you put some old notions about work to sleep, you will come into your own as a person. Regardless of your position in life, you will enjoy your leisure more by having a positive perspective about how being without work can add to the quality of your life.

> Work: The thing that interferes with golf.
> —Frank Dane

Exercise 3-1. Something to Think About

As I mentioned in Chapter 2, your ability to enjoy spare time will, in part, depend on how open-minded you are. To challenge your values and attitudes about work, answer the following questions:

Do you believe that hard work is the key to success in this world? Why?

Do you think that it is productive for North American society to have every able person between the ages of sixteen and sixty-five years old gainfully employed at least forty hours a week?

Are unemployed panhandlers a drain on society?

There are no right answers to the above questions. This chapter is meant to challenge your beliefs and values associated with work and leisure. I hope the following content will divert your thinking in other directions than it might normally take.

The Protestant Work Ethic Ruined a Good Thing

Contrary to common beliefs, the work ethic isn't a traditional value. In fact, most of our ancestors would have rejected this notion. So who is the culprit who invented work and the work ethic? The work ethic arrived with the Industrial Revolution. Working long hours started with the factory system. Over time, the number of regular hours in a work-week fell from sixty hours in 1890 to about forty hours in 1950. Since then, regular work hours haven't declined significantly. The effects of the work ethic introduced by the Industrial Revolution are still with us.

Anyone with a part-time job isn't considered a contributing member of society. Even though many people could forgo a reduction in pay to work shorter hours, some will not do so given the opportunity because they would feel guilty working shorter hours.

Let's go back in history to a time when people looked at work in a different light. Ancient Greeks thought work was vulgar. Work, just for the sake of work, signified slavery and a lack of productivity. The only reason for work was to acquire more leisure. Socrates stated that because manual laborers had no time for friendship or for serving the community, they made bad citizens and undesirable friends. The early Greeks and Romans relegated all activities done with the hands, done under orders, or done for wages to the lower-class citizens or to the slaves. The early Greeks didn't even have a term to describe what we call work today.

> The best test of the quality of a civilization is the quality of its leisure.
>
> —Irwin Edman

Likewise, the early Europeans didn't have a term for work as we know it today. Although European peasants in the Middle Ages were poor and oppressed, they didn't work long hours. They celebrated holidays in the honor of even the most obscure saints; consequently, with time, they had more holidays and fewer and fewer workdays. The normal number of holidays at one time was 115 a year. Then along came the work ethic to eliminate all these holidays.

To the early Greeks, leisure wasn't just a rest from work; it was desirable as an end in itself. As should be the case, leisure time was the most productive time. One could use this time to think, learn, and develop the self. If one believes there is no greater goal for sophisticated people than to grow and become self-actualized, ancient Greeks seemed to have their thinking in order.

Then along came the Protestant work ethic to ruin this perfectly intelligent way to think about work. For some strange reason, society took a wrong turn and adopted the new work ethic. This change reversed the roles for work and leisure. Work became the productive activity. Leisure was to be used only for allowing individuals to rest, so they could be more effective in the workplace.

This "modern" mode of thinking now relies on guilt to make it more effective. Guilt—in a perverse way—nullifies pleasure. These negative emotions are so strong for many people that feelings of guilt surface even when they go on vacations. Unable to enjoy their time off, these bubbleheads come back from their vacations having attained negative emotional benefits.

This is the North American way: The majority view work with such respect that they boast about how many hours a day they work. Even if the job is routine and tiresome and the financial gain from working overtime is zero, these people can't resist bragging about how hard they have been working. They have become martyrs, giving up the

> There is no more fatal blunderer than he who consumes the greater part of his life getting his living.
> —Henry David Thoreau

opportunity for self-actualization in return for the privilege of being slaves, primarily benefiting the company rather than themselves.

Today, influenced by the work ethic, many people exaggerate or lie about how much they actually work. In 1995, researchers discovered that people actually worked less than they, themselves, estimated. When the researchers compared the actual hours recorded in time diaries to the workers' previous estimates, they found a significant gap between the estimates and the actual time worked. Extreme workaholics had the biggest difference; they said they worked seventy-five-hour weeks when, in fact, the diaries showed they only worked fifty hours a week.

With the reversal in the roles of work and leisure, work has become the sole organizing principle and means for expression. In the modern world, leisure has a much lower status than work. To many people, leisure represents idleness and a waste of valuable time. Without work, many people exhibit a deterioration in their personalities and a loss in self-esteem. New faults, such as drinking and unfaithfulness, appear in many individuals when they lose their jobs.

Modern technology in Western societies has made it possible for leisure to be a privilege for many different people in the community, not only for aristocrats. I am sure the progressive philosophers in ancient Greece would be greatly confused to learn that many people in the modern world, having more leisure than ever before, are not quite sure what to do with their extra time. The Greeks would be most perplexed by today's individuals who work long hours even though they are financially well-off.

> Let us be grateful to Adam: he cut us out of the blessing of idleness and won for us the curse of labor.
> —Mark Twain

I am not quite sure what has caused society to accept the reversal in the roles of work and leisure and the effects of such a reversal. There is one thing I am sure about: The ancient Greeks would not only be confused, but disgusted with the progress in humankind. To them, it would appear that many people in modern American society either have serious kinks in their brains, or they have developed masochistic tendencies.

Don't Work Because It's Moral to Do So

Working at an unpleasant job when it is necessary for one's survival is rational. Working at an unpleasant job when one is financially well-off and doesn't have to work is irrational. Nevertheless, many well-off people toil away at unpleasant jobs because they believe it is moral to be working.

> Don't be too moral. You may cheat yourself out of life so.
> —Henry David Thoreau

Most people haven't stopped to consider that a great deal of harm may result from adopting the belief that work is a virtue. Although work is necessary for our survival, it doesn't contribute as much to individual well-being as many think it contributes.

Just to set things straight, I am not saying that we should avoid as much work as possible. You may have erroneously assumed I suffer from ergophobia (the fear of work). On the contrary, I get a great deal of satisfaction from the work I choose. Writing this book is one example.

My point is that working for the sake of working can be detrimental to our well-being and our enjoyment of life. This is by no means a new revelation. Bertrand Russell, some time ago, stated that North America's attitude toward work and leisure was outdated and contributed to the misery in society. In his essay, "In Praise Of Idleness," Russell stated: "The morality of work is the morality of slaves, and the modern world has no need of slavery."

I would like you to believe that Bertrand borrowed this line from me, but this would sound far-fetched, considering he wrote this in 1932, over sixty years ago. Reading Russell's essay today is eye-opening because of its relevance in this day and age. Although our world has dramatically changed, it is interesting to see how little our values have changed in over sixty years. Old values and beliefs are hard to surrender.

All keeping my nose to the grindstone for twenty-five years has given me is a sore nose.

Let us use an example to illustrate the ludicrous results that can occur from hanging on to the belief that hard work is a virtue. Now, assume at any given moment the world needs X number of paper clips for its operations. With conventional technology, Y number of people are needed to produce these paper clips. They all work ten hours a day, and everyone wishes they had more leisure time. Suppose someone invents a new and more efficient machine for making paper clips, allowing half as many people as before to produce X number of paper clips. In a sensible world, the paper-clip makers would all work half as many hours as they worked before. They would all have much more leisure time.

The world is not this sensible. Because people still hang on to the belief that they should all work ten hours a day, all paper-clip makers work these hours until there is a surplus in paper clips. Eventually, half of the workers are laid off. This guarantees everyone is miserable. The laid-off workers have too much leisure time and not enough money. The retained workers are overworked and have too little spare time.

Hard work never killed anybody, but why take a chance?
—Charlie McCarthy (Edgar Bergen)

Instead of contributing to everyone's happiness, the unavoidable increase in leisure adds to everyone's misery. The morality of work ends up greatly increasing unhappiness. Only by having our morals change to keep pace with our changing world can we avoid these unhealthy situations.

The Law of Detrimental Returns

In North America, hard work is supposed to be the key to success. Contrary to popular belief, this is seldom the case. For some mysterious reason, people who espouse the virtues of hard work in our society overlook the fact that several million people keep their noses to the grindstone throughout their careers and wind up with nothing but flat noses. They certainly don't fulfill their dreams.

Because a certain amount of work is good for us, it doesn't automatically follow that twice as much work should be twice as good for us.

The law of diminishing returns takes over after a certain point. We gain less and less for each extra hour that we work.

No man who is in a hurry is quite civilized.
—Will Durant

Things go from bad to worse. After the point of diminishing returns, we can reach another point. We reach what I call the law of detrimental returns. Any extra work after this level will actually subtract from our overall enjoyment of life. Additional time spent at work contributes to the many undesirable consequences associated with mental and physical ailments.

A Nation Gone Mad with the Work Ethic

Can you imagine this? Everyone in the nation loves working more than anything else. The work ethic gets so out of hand that factory workers, even though they are entitled to only seven days' annual vacation, routinely refuse to take their entire vacations, preferring instead to stay at the plant and work.

The whole nation has gone mad. Businesspeople, like everyone else, still insist on working six days a week. Although they are entitled to twenty days vacation, they take no more vacation than factory workers. When businesspeople take vacations, they don't know how to relax. Instead, they behave like maniacs, rushing back and forth, exhausting themselves trying to get in as much leisure as possible. They are so brainwashed with the work ethic that they don't quite know what leisure is. Things get so bad that health in the nation starts to suffer. The government eventually steps in with programs to teach people how to have more leisure.

Imagine the Human Resources Department in Canada or the Department of Labor in the United States promoting more leisure. This would be severely criticized in either country. However, the situation described above is real; it is happening in Japan.

The Japanese government, with its long-term focus, has made one of its objectives the improvement of the quality of life by increasing leisure. Through the Japanese Ministry of Labor, the government has created a poster series promoting more time off for workers. One such poster says, "Let's realize a five-day workweek society." The ministry also publishes a handbook under the title *Try Your Best: Salaryman's Guide to Relaxation.* It gives workers ideas on how to take time off.

Just watching people work makes me tired. Thanks to the two of you for working harder than the Japanese, I am now terribly exhausted and have to go home early for my afternoon nap.

Nearly two thirds of Japanese people taking part in a survey said they take less than ten vacation days a year. However, many workers would like more time off. Guess what most wanted to do with more leisure? More than 85 percent just wanted to sleep more. One would have to surmise that they are either extremely tired from overwork, or the work ethic has made them a very boring society.

Undoubtedly, the Japanese have a difficult time accepting the concept of not working. When Tokyo's Kodansha Publishing, the largest book publisher in Japan, decided to publish *The Joy of Not Working,* the editors had a difficult time deciding on the title for the Japanese version. They felt that anything in Japanese close to the English title was too radical for Japanese citizens, especially older ones. Kodansha's editors eventually decided to call the book *Zelinski's Law,* playing on *Murphy's Law,* which was a big seller in its Japanese version. (*Zelinski's Law* has a subtitle that, translated into English, says *The Book that Will Make You Not Want to Work Ever Again.*)

Hard Work Is a Killer

Many Japanese are not only tired, but exhausted from overwork. A survey conducted by the Fukoku Life Insurance Company of Japan reported nearly half of Japan's salaried employees fear that their jobs will drive them to an early death.

Japan's work ethic is so strong that they have even developed a disease to go along with it. *Karoshi* is the Japanese term for sudden death from overwork. Reports indicate 10 percent of male fatalities are attributed to overwork. Families are now successfully suing companies for contributing to the deaths of loved ones. In 1996, Dentsu, Japan's largest advertising agency, was ordered by a Japanese court to pay the equivalent of 1.2 million U.S. dollars to the parents of a man who committed suicide because of chronic overwork and a lack of sleep.

Death is nature's way of telling us to slow down.
—Graffiti in washroom

Personally, I feel individuals, whether Japanese, American, or Canadian, who die from overwork have no one to blame but themselves. Anyone crazy enough to work that hard, when there are so many wonderful things to do in life, will get little sympathy from me. Furthermore, I don't know why Japan had to come up with another term for this disease. They already had one; the term *hara-kiri* would have done nicely.

Bart Simpson's Philosophy Brings Hope

Like young American adults, young Japanese adults are showing more sanity than their elders when it comes to the work ethic. Values are changing for the better in both nations.

A reflection of the changing values can be seen on Japan's hottest TV program in the early 1990s. Chibi Marukochan, Japan's version of Bart Simpson, is a girl who has been getting top TV billing all over the nation. She has charmed children and adults alike, especially adult women between twenty and twenty-five. Two in five TV sets tune to this Sunday cartoon showing Chibi as a relentlessly mediocre third grader who growls and avoids work as much as possible.

The work ethic is now seen as a sham by many young adults in Japan. They are even more likely than American youth to question dedication to work. The new generation, or *shinjinrui*, also have little interest in dedicating themselves to working for only one company, as their parents did. Younger Japanese adults, like their American counterparts, not only want a more intelligent lifestyle, they are demanding it. *Newsweek,* in March 1996, reported that even many Japanese adults have had enough. The magazine stated that the modern Japanese company man "takes vacations. He spends off-hours with friends, not his boss. He may even get home to tuck in his kids."

Loafing Is for High Achievers

Many great achievers in the history of humankind have been lazy according to their societys' standards. Although this sounds like a contradiction, great achievers spent a lot of time avoiding work. They weren't necessarily lazy, but the majority in society, probably somewhat due to envy, viewed them as such.

Being creative loafers, these achievers spent considerable time relaxing and thinking. A creative loafer is one who accomplishes something significant but doesn't overdo it with sustained activity. Creative loafing results in relaxed but productive activity.

Although they didn't work long hours, many achievers through the ages were highly efficient and productive when they worked on their imaginative and valuable projects. Of course,

> It is better to have loafed and lost than never to have loafed at all.
> —James Thurber

because they took time to loaf, they were more relaxed, happier, and healthier than they would have been if they had overworked themselves.

Why Panhandlers Contribute to Society

One day, I emphatically stated to a friend that I often contribute to charities, but I won't give money to panhandlers. I let her know that I thought panhandlers are lazy degenerates who serve no purpose, except to harass me while I am walking down the street, on my merry way to a favorite bistro.

This friend quickly gave me a lesson in one of my seminar topics: the ability to be flexible in one's thinking. Someone once said we teach best those things we need to know; there may be some truth to this.

My friend informed me that panhandlers, because of their lifestyle, utilize few resources and aren't a drain on the environment as are working people. Panhandlers don't steal for their money, but ask for it. They make certain donors happy by giving them the opportunity to help someone. Also, in a world where full employment becomes less likely with time, every panhandler not working in the system means one less person competing for a valuable job.

As I reflected upon this, it occurred to me that some working people I know are more degenerate than panhandlers, and don't make as many contributions to society. I no longer get upset when I

I always wanted to be a degenerate panhandler, but I couldn't quite make it. That's why I got myself an office job.

encounter panhandlers. Occasionally, I give them money and think about their great contributions to society. Other times, I beat them to the punch and ask them for money first. In this way, I may be able to make the same contributions as they make to society.

To Be a Yuppie Is to Be a Successful Failure

There are two things phonier than a three-dollar bill: One is a tree filled with elephants; the other is a successful yuppie. During the 1980s, and into the early 1990s, yuppies, with their paste-on smiles and masks of false happiness, lived Halloween 365 days a year.

Yuppies, in their madness, made the work ethic trendy. With hard work was supposed to come incredible success and the good life. Being a yuppie meant it was easier and better to be recognized for what one owned than for whom one was.

The world yuppies inhabited, and to which many others still aspire, isn't all it's cracked up to be. Due to their wealth-warped mentalities and addictions to overwork, yuppies in great numbers suffered from hypertension, ulcers, heart disease, alcohol abuse, and drug dependence. To cope with this, many yuppies—some just to keep up with the latest trends—were seeing therapists. There were specialist therapists for lawyers, specialist therapists for doctors, and even specialist therapists for yuppie therapists.

When it comes to leisure time, North American yuppies were not much better off than the Japanese. Despite their abundant salaries, yuppies found leisure time the hardest thing to buy. According to a Harris survey, the amount of leisure time enjoyed by the average American shrank 37 percent since 1973. Yuppies, with their long work days, had their spare time shrink even more than the average. For many of these young urban professionals, life became so harried that even leisure, if it was fitted in at all, was done according to schedule.

Many children in yuppie families missed their childhood because their parents were too busy chasing money, material goods, and status. Some yuppies arranged to meet their children sometime during the week by making appointments with them. Other yuppies were training their children from an early

Harold, it's been ten years since we were in the MBA program at Stanford. What in the world are you doing driving cabs?

I used to be a successful yuppie, but I gave up my nervous twitches, paste-on smile, and therapist, and it ruined my career.

age to be "successful" like them. Their children's schedules were so filled up with activities that they never learned what it is like to just relax and "do nothing."

In light of all these complications, people who chose a yuppie lifestyle and are still trying to maintain it at all costs certainly don't appear to be rational people brimming over with sensible thoughts. Although they boasted about how hard they worked, they don't appear to have had many overworked brain cells. Pamela Ennis, an industrial psychologist based in Toronto who counseled many yuppies laid off in the early 1990s, was quoted in *Report on Business* magazine: "This generation has a screw loose. They don't understand that a condo in Collingwood or a BMW is not going to bring them satisfaction."

The success that yuppies strived for was self-defeating. Considering all their attendant problems, we should have more appropriately called them yuffies (young urban failures) rather than yuppies.

Is Your Life All about Stuff?

As ridiculous as it seems, our primary purpose in life, as defined by our society, is to acquire material goods using the monetary fruits of our work. Yuppies have undertaken this purpose to the extreme. The rest of us are not much better; we have not stopped to think about our real purpose in life.

George Carlin's comedy act about stuff says a lot. I don't recall exactly how he says it, but it goes something like this: Right from the time we are young we are given stuff.

All my possessions for a moment of time.

—Queen Elizabeth I

We learn to like stuff. As we grow up, we want even more stuff. We continually ask our parents for money, so we can buy stuff. Then when we are of age, we get a job to buy stuff. We purchase a house in which we put our stuff. Needless to say, we must buy a car to haul our stuff around. Because we soon acquire too much stuff, our house becomes too small. So we get a bigger house. Now we don't have enough stuff for the big house, so we buy more stuff. We need a new car because we have worn out our old car carrying this stuff around. And on it goes. But, we never get all the stuff we want.

All this stuff about stuff is funny, but at the same time dismaying. It shows how our addiction to working supports our addiction to getting more and more stuff, much of which we definitely don't need.

What the "G" in GNP Really Stands For

Economists, businesspeople, and politicians tell us we will all be better off if our countries have substantial increases in the gross national product (GNP). Gross national product is the value of all services and products sold in a country during any given year. It is the measurement that tells us if we have been successful as a nation. The wise men and women of business and economics tell us that the goal in any country's economy is growth in GNP.

If all economists were laid end to end, they would not reach a conclusion.

—George Bernard Shaw

Another goal for the economy is to eliminate unemployment. The ability to generate new jobs is dependent on economic growth. A certain level of GNP is supposed to provide jobs for everyone able to work, whether they want to work or not.

Having taught economics courses at private vocational schools and universities, I have always had a problem with GNP as a yardstick of prosperity. GNP is improved by increases in such questionable activities as consumption of cigarettes and the production of weapons. A substantial increase in car accidents will favorably affect GNP because more funerals, hospital visits, car repairs, and new car purchases will result.

If all economists were laid end to end, it would not be a bad idea.
—Unknown Wise Person

With the growth in GNP considered such an important yardstick, it surprises me that the skipper on the *Exxon Valdez* didn't receive a Nobel Prize for economics. The gross national product in the United States increased by $1.7 billion due to the Exxon oil spill. More such massive oil spills would do wonders for the GNP. Lots more people would also be employed.

Growth in GNP for the sake of growth doesn't necessarily reflect something beneficial to society. Growth for the sake of growth is also the philosophy of cancer cells. Instead of standing for the gross national product, GNP should stand for the grossness of the national product.

The True Measure of a Nation's Success

Recently, I talked to a couple who had traveled extensively. They were fortunate to meet the king of Bhutan. As a country, Bhutan is relatively undeveloped. The people are poor, but not poverty stricken. Nevertheless, the people in the country are content with their state in life.

Much happiness is lost in the pursuit of it.
—Unknown Wise Person

When the couple asked about Bhutan's low gross national product, the king replied, "We don't believe in gross national product; we believe in gross national happiness."

So how about this folks? Let's use gross national happiness (GNH) rather than GNP to measure how well the countries of the world are doing. We can probably create a more workable world, but first we must find out how to eliminate all the economists.

Taking It Easy for the Environment

Caring for the environment has become a topic of paramount importance. Yet few people are willing to admit that their own wealth-warped values and excessive drive for success contribute to serious environmental pollution. If people were to take it easy and work less, they would help create a greener world.

This is dependent upon the utilization of natural resources. Any use of natural resources contributes to pollution in our environment. Most increases in GNP are at a substantial cost to our environment.

For a greener planet, we must reduce our use of natural resources. We in North America can probably get by with half the resources we use and still maintain a good standard of living. This can be accomplished, in part, by changing our values. We must eliminate frivolous work and consumption, such as the production of stupid trinkets and gadgets that people buy and use for a week or two before throwing away.

More than a hundred years ago, John Stuart Mill predicted that if the world continued on its path of economic growth, the environment would be totally destroyed. His premise was that wealth, as defined by Western nations, is dependent upon defacing the environment. As some of us are now aware, the environment cannot withstand the increasing demands we have placed on it. Our addiction to excessive materialism must be cured. Most economists and businesspeople see leisure as positive only if we have money, and we use it to buy more leisure items and services. Money has its limitations, as stated by John Kenneth Galbraith, the well-known economist, who views money and consumption in a different light than do most economists:

> Millions long for immortality who don't know what to do on a rainy Sunday afternoon.
> —Susan Ertz

> I am not quite sure what the advantage is in having a few more dollars to spend if the air is too dirty to breathe, the water too polluted to drink, the commuters are losing out in the struggle to get in and out of the city, the streets are filthy and the schools so bad that the young perhaps wisely stay away, and the hoodlums roll citizens for some of the dollars they saved in the tax cut.

Saving our planet will require more than recycling bottles and cans. There is something ridiculous about producing unnecessary trinkets and various other products just to keep people busy working. It is apparent that individuals who are able to take it easy, work less, and consume less are making an important contribution to a greener world.

Towards Less Work and Better Living

The work ethic may be doing us more harm than good. We have to discard our work-focused and wealth-warped mentalities if we are to understand what is really important for our happiness. Studs Terkel, in his book *Working*, stated that the time has come to revise the work ethic. Many modern North American beliefs make people slaves when they don't have to be. The concept of work, as we know it, is long overdue for review.

The modest values from the eighteenth century are more appropriate for today than the twentieth-century values we have adopted. We lost the sense of moderation in the 1980s. Most of us cherished the Donald Trump values of habitual striving for more and bigger stuff.

Sometimes I get an irresistible urge to work hard like you two guys, but I just lie down until the feeling goes away, and then I'm okay.

For the late 1990s and beyond into the new millennium, the profile of the eighteenth-century gentleman, who made his modest amount of money and then retired to more worthwhile pursuits, makes greater sense than the Trump style. An inner world of personal growth, replacing the external world of material growth, will contribute to greater satisfaction and well-being.

Less emphasis on the need to be working and on the obsession with stuff is in order. Working for a living is necessary, but not to the

> The end of labor is to gain leisure.
> —Aristotle

degree most people think. Introducing more modest material goals will do wonders for our environment and give us the opportunity to enjoy a more leisurely lifestyle.

The Real Stuff of Life

The comments in the previous sections emphasize a few shortcomings of the values dear to North American society. If you have blindly adopted these values, challenging them and seeing things differently can add to the quality of your life. Having strict beliefs that work is virtuous and play is frivolous will impair your ability to respond to periods of unemployment and retirement. If you are working, these same values may leave you unfulfilled because of an imbalance in your lifestyle.

Being more open-minded and placing less emphasis on the value of the work ethic and materialism has its merits. Working less can have many payoffs. Time away from the workplace, no matter what your situation, can be an opportunity to learn in new ways and grow as a person. Someone who works long hours and owns many gadgets, trinkets, and other "stuff" isn't a better person than the individual who works fewer hours and owns less. The addiction to stuff tends to alienate us from other people and the environment.

That sounds like a real good trade.

Guess what? Today I am getting an expensive set of golf clubs for my husband.

In the higher order of life, all the different kinds of stuff around us—cars, houses, stereos, jobs—are conveniences and nothing else. They aren't the source of our happiness. The things we own, the places we live, and the jobs we have are secondary in importance. True success shouldn't be measured by what we own or what we do for a living. Our real essence is of a higher order. The only important things, in the end, are related to how well we are living today: what are we learning, how much are we laughing and playing, and how much love do we show for the world around us. This is the real stuff of life!

CHAPTER 4

Working Less, Just for the Health of It

The Trap with No Cheese

If we experiment with a rat by consistently placing cheese in the third of several tunnels, the rat will eventually figure out the cheese is always in the third tunnel. The rat will go directly to the third tunnel without looking in the other tunnels. However, if we start putting the cheese in the sixth tunnel, the rat will keep on going to the third tunnel for only so long. Sooner or later, the rat will realize there is no cheese in the third tunnel; the rat will now start looking in the other tunnels until it discovers the cheese is in the sixth tunnel. The rat will now consistently show up in the tunnel with the cheese.

> *I don't want the cheese, I just want to get out of the trap.*
> *—Spanish Proverb*

The difference between a rat and a person is that the majority of people will remain in a tunnel when it is obvious there is no cheese in it. Most human beings get themselves into traps from which they never escape. It's pretty hard to get the cheese when one is caught in a trap that has no cheese left or, in some cases, had no cheese in it in the first place.

"Cheese" here represents happiness, satisfaction, and fulfillment. Today unhappiness in great measure exists in the ranks of most management circles. This is a contention by Jan Halper, a Palo Alto psychologist and management consultant who spent ten years exploring the careers and emotions of over 4000 male executives. Halper found many men in management appeared to be happy, but were just the opposite. Of those in middle management, 58 percent felt they had wasted many years of their lives while struggling to achieve their goals. They were bitter about the many sacrifices they made during these years. These men weren't doing what they should have been doing to have a balanced life. Other research shows up to 70 percent of white-collar workers are unhappy with their jobs. Ironically, a majority of white-collar workers are dissatisfied with their jobs, but they are spending more and more time working.

There is more to life than increasing its speed.
—Mohandas K. Gandhi

We use the term "being in the rat race," but it isn't an appropriate one—it is demeaning to rats. Rats won't stay in a tunnel without cheese. It would be more appropriate for rats to use the term "being in the human race," when they find themselves doing ridiculous things like going down the same tunnel without finding any cheese.

Reading more material from this chapter isn't necessary if you are a rat or a mentally and financially prosperous human being who isn't working and doesn't intend to work for the rest of your life. However, this chapter may be valuable if you are still working at a job, or if you are unemployed and plan to go back to work sometime in the future. Jobs don't always provide all the different types of cheese people are looking for. Tunnel vision and ignorance are two big hindrances for human beings trying to attain satisfaction and fulfillment in their lives. This chapter is intended to help you avoid the traps that appear in many jobs. It is also designed to help put some balance in your life and prepare you for the time when you retire from work.

Do You Know Who You Are?

To help you get a proper perspective on who you are and whether you are a workaholic, here is simple exercise.

Exercise 4-1. A Simple Question?

Take a few moments in answering this simple question:
  Who are you?

When attempting the above exercise, practically all working people will write down what they do for a living or what nationality they are, what religion they follow, whether they are married, where they live, and how old they are. What people do for a living is the thing on which they usually focus. Few people associate interests away from the job with their identity. This reveals that most people's identities are tied to their jobs.

One of the symptoms of an approaching nervous breakdown is the belief that one's work is terribly important.
—Bertrand Russell

In today's generation, managers have invested a lot, emotionally and financially, in their careers; their sense of identity comes from their skills and talents. Corporate America has been telling us we build our character by working and doing "productive" things in organizations. We have learned to define ourselves by our jobs. There is something seriously wrong with this: If we think we are what we do for a living, we have lost most of our character.

How much of your identity is tied to your job? If you are a lawyer who has become so immersed in your job that all your identity is tied to it, you will answer that you are a lawyer in response to "Who are you?" That is exactly what all other lawyers who tie most of their identity to their jobs will say in answer to this question. If your identity is mainly tied to your job, you may be limiting yourself as a person. Unless you love your job so much that you are totally blown away by it, your job should comprise only a minute part of your identity.

When you put all your life into a job, there is the danger it will chip away at your personality until there is nothing left. Your occupation shouldn't be who you are. An occupation is what you do to earn money. Who you are should be your essence. Your essence is your character and your individuality. Those qualities and elements are what make you different from other people.

Yes, this job will definitely enhance my identity. If I get it, my BMW won't be repossessed.

To find out who you are, look inside yourself for your own decisions, tastes, and interests. Don't let work become the only thing with meaning. Ensure that you develop hobbies and interests, aside from work, that have just as much, or more, meaning than your job. Your self-image will then be something other than just your job. Listen to the intuitive voices within yourself, and not the logical voices in your organization, the establishment, or society. The best place to display your uniqueness is in your personal life. When you are asked who you are, most of your identity should be associated with your essence, which you display in pursuing personal interests in your leisure time.

Ignorance Runs Rampant in Today's Corporate World

In today's world, outmoded attitudes and values cherished by many corporate executives help to perpetuate a work environment characterized by workaholism. This is damaging employees' health. Ignorance, at all levels, including the higher echelons in management, runs rampant in major corporations across North America. Comfortable in this sea of ignorance, workaholics are not only tolerated, but respected. Because workaholism is about greed and power, many business leaders love workaholics. In many departments, where in numerous cases most workers can be classified as workaholics, it's fashionable to put in sixty to eighty hours a week. It's also fashionable to be in a hurry and be overextended in one's work. Some managers even feel heroic when overcommitted all of the time.

Ignorance is never out of style. It was in fashion yesterday, it is the rage today, and it will set the pace tomorrow.
—Frank Dane

This situation has serious implications: Workaholics are no different from any other addicts. All addicts are neurotics with serious problems. Workaholics, like alcoholics, are in a state of denial about the existence of their problem but still suffer from the serious consequences arising from the addiction. The same is true with people who support addicts; they are no better than addicts, neurotics at best.

Why do corporations support addiction? Anne Wilson Schaef explains this in great detail in her book *When Society Becomes an Addict.* She states that addictive behavior is the norm in American society. Society itself functions as an addict, as do a lot of organizations. In her later book, *The Addictive Organization,* Schaef and her coauthor, Diane Fassel, go into great detail about why most large organizations are affected by addictions and function like addictive individuals.

To serve their own interests, corporations have encouraged and promoted workaholism. Under the guise of quality and excellence, the corporate work ethic places the corporation ahead of everything else. The emphasis on the company's drive for success means it shouldn't matter if an individual's physical or mental health is wiped out or his or her marriage is ruined.

Promoting the importance of work and emphasizing the need to be in a hurry go hand in hand with promoting productivity. In reality, this only appears to promote productivity. Having company employees work longer, harder, and faster, while sacrificing their leisure time, doesn't necessarily mean more will be

> He worked like hell in the country so he could live in the city, where he worked like hell so he could live in the country.
> —Don Marquis

accomplished in the organization. In fact, the result can be quite the contrary. Less will be accomplished in the long run, because productivity and efficiency will sooner or later suffer from the decreased effectiveness of workers suffering from stress and burnout. It is interesting that strong-willed individuals are more likely to burn out than "wimps," because the strength possessed by the strong-willed is based on denial.

Employees with no time to think, making careless mistakes, can cause the organization to be less innovative and less productive in the long run. Contrary to popular belief, always being in a hurry to get something done is not productive. A frantic routine leaves no time for just thinking. Creativity doesn't flow if not enough time is made available for it. A productive and successful worker needs the time to sit back, ponder the big picture, and take the long-term view.

The detrimental consequences of the mad world of corporate life are far-reaching. In the frenzy of hard work and day-to-day survival, many people have lost their personal dreams and zest for living. Deprived family and social lives result from overwork and stress. For those feeling burnout, there is no more purpose, meaning, and vigor in living.

If we look back in time to ancient Greece, the modern workaholic yuppie seems like another case of history (along with ignorance) repeating itself. Plato, in early Greece, criticized those people ignorant and foolhardy enough to evade leisure by working too much. He warned them about getting caught up in luxury, power, reputation, influence, and excessive amusements. Viewing work as the center of existence was to be avoided. Plato felt that people who kept working after they had met their basic needs, were missing out on more important pursuits.

Go to Jail and Live Longer

Your high-stress job may do you more harm than you ever imagined. It may even lower your IQ. A recent research study led researchers to conclude that prolonged exposure to stress can speed up the aging in brain cells and interfere with learning and memory. Long-term memory may actually be decreased with the damage to brain cells from the effects of stress.

If you want to escape the stress common in the modern work world and increase your health and longevity at the same time, try robbing a bank or two. Make sure you get caught in the act. Jail may be the best place for you if you want to escape stress. Researchers at the Institute Bustave Roussy in Villejuif, France, have discovered that French prisoners live longer and have lower rates of disease, including cancer and heart disease, than other Frenchmen. The longer they stayed in jail, the lower was their death rate. Why? It certainly has nothing to do with the use of alcohol, cigarettes, or drugs, which are used by most prisoners. The researchers postulate that prison life is simply less stressful than normal life. Prisoners have a more leisurely lifestyle than the general population.

By working faithfully eight hours a day you may eventually get to be a boss and work twelve hours a day.
—Robert Frost

The French prisoners are onto something. They have found a way to escape work and get more leisure in their lives. You may want to commit some crime, get caught at it, and go to jail. More leisure will improve your health and increase your longevity. Of course, going to jail isn't the only way to create more leisure in your life.

Crazy George Is Not That Crazy

Most work in which people engage is routine and tiresome. Millions in North America want to flee from their jobs but can't figure out where to go. These people should talk to my friend, who is known to us as Crazy George. He may be a great role model. We call George "crazy" because he is different. One different thing about George is he doesn't like working for organizations. He considers it demeaning to his character. George does not relish having others tell him what to do, how to do it, and what time to come to work. George either doesn't care for or despises many other characteristics of the typical workplace.

Living on the fringes, he does a little work here and there. Crazy George is seldom in a rush. He has been a third-year apprentice carpenter for something like fourteen years and never seems to last on any one job for more than a month or two. His personal record for the shortest time on any particular job is five minutes. He also does some freelance auto bodywork. His income is often below the poverty line; however, because he spends money only on the basics, George has managed to put away more money in the bank than many people who make $75,000 or more a year.

The interesting thing about Crazy George is he is over fifty years old and looks like he is in his late thirties. On the other hand, I know "successful" working people who are in their late thirties and look like they are over fifty. George looks much younger than his age because of his healthy lifestyle. Like the French prisoners, he doesn't have to contend with the stresses to which the masses are subjected. If Crazy George maintains his condition, he will be able to work in his eighties if he has to. Because he has his freedom as well, Crazy George is even better off than the French prisoners. Considering all factors, I contend that Crazy George isn't that crazy; the employed who indulge in excessive work are the crazy ones.

Leisure Is In; Workaholism Is Passé

In the 1980s, millions of North Americans made work the center of their existence. By doing so, they distorted their lives and fell into emotional turmoil. The road to corporate success left many feeling hollow and shallow. Yesterday's dreams became today's nightmares. Many people realized they were slaves to their jobs and their possessions. Spending fifty to eighty hours a week at the workplace contributed to a loss of self. Totally focusing on their work destroyed what essence many people once had. To make matters worse, job stress and burnout robbed them of their physical and mental well-being. They paid a big price for their involvement in voluntary slavery.

The good news is that "the times, they are a-changing." As the world entered the 1990s, many employees started looking at work in a different light. For the first time in fifteen years, working Americans said leisure—instead of work—is the important thing in their lives. A total of 41 percent of respondents to the 1990 poll conducted

> I have never liked working. To me a job is an invasion of privacy.
> —Danny McGoorty

by the Roper Organization chose leisure as the most important element in their lives, while only 36 percent chose work. This is a significant statistic. In 1985, work came out ahead of leisure by a score of 46 percent to 33 percent.

Studies suggest an increasing number of North Americans have a hunger for quiet and unhurried living. Refugees from stress and burnout are starting to leave organizations in droves. The 1990s have become the decade for employees to try to get away from the madness at work, either by leaving work completely, or by adopting alternative work arrangements to create a better balance between work and leisure. Several newspapers have reported that workaholism is passé. Leisure is in; free time is the ultimate status symbol for the 1990s.

> America has become so tense and nervous it has been years since I've seen anyone sleep in church—and that is a sad situation.
>
> —Norman Vincent Peale

Even some organizations have seen the light; quality leisure in employees' lives contributes to the health of the organization. Many companies are discovering that healthy employees are happier and more productive. Considering that 80 percent of illness is attributed to lifestyle-related causes, it should be no surprise that companies are interested in employees' health and morale improvements gained from increased enjoyment of leisure activities. The result for the organization can be a tremendous payoff in productivity, stamina, motivation, and good corporate image. Several major corporations have adopted training programs to promote wellness and a balanced lifestyle for their employees.

In the future, organizations will have no alternative. Employees will demand a better balance between work and leisure. Unlike the baby boomers, today's recruits aren't as likely to be workaholics lured by the trappings of money, title, security, and ladder climbing. They have a new attitude towards life and work. In the mid-1990s, magazines such as *Fortune* are reporting that generation Xers are focusing on quality of life—job satisfaction versus pay.

> Personally, I have nothing against work, particularly when performed quietly and unobtrusively by someone else.
>
> —Barbara Ehrenreich

USA TODAY, in April 1996, reported that 55 percent of baby boomers in the United States express themselves through their work. This compares with 46 percent for members of generation X. As should be, employees in their twenties and thirties say leisure, lifestyle, and family are at least as important as work. Personally, I am happy about the change in values; the present generation has more wholesome values than baby boomers, who think their jobs are their lives.

Leisure Lovers May Help Reduce Unemployment

More people focusing on the quality of life and leisure may in the long run benefit not only those having more leisure time; this may also benefit people who have too much leisure and not enough work. A 1996 study by Robert Half International found that men and women in the United States are willing to take bigger cuts in working hours and pay to spend time with their families than they were in 1989. Almost two thirds of workers are willing to reduce hours and pay—the average reduction they would accept is 21 percent. A similar poll in 1989 found that about the same number of respondents were willing to decrease hours and salary by an average of 13 percent to spend more time with family.

With more employed people working fewer hours for less pay, new possibilities are opened up for the unemployed. Frank Reid, a University of Toronto economist, quoted in an article in *Western Living* magazine, stated that 500,000 new jobs could be created in Canada by letting those who want to work less do so and turning this extra work over to the unemployed. Correspondingly, in the United States, the number of new jobs created could be as high as several million.

> We are always getting ready to live, but not really living.
> —Ralph Waldo Emerson

Unfortunately, organizational and societal rigidity towards adopting new employment options is creating barriers to opening up this opportunity for reducing unemployment. Let's hope these barriers will be removed in the near future. With these barriers gone many employed and many unemployed individuals will be happier because they will have a better balance in their lives.

To Be a Peak Performer, Work Less and Play More

Reading a fiction thriller, working in the garden, or just daydreaming while lying in the hammock are ways to increase your productivity at work. If you want to be a peak performer at your job, try working less and playing more. A generous amount of leisure in your life will increase your wealth. I am talking about mental wealth. In the long run, you will likely also increase your financial wealth if you take more time for leisure.

Indulging in more leisure-time interests and hobbies has many benefits. Hobbies and interests outside your work help you to be more innovative in your job. While you are engaged in leisurely pursuits, your conscious mind takes a rest from your work-related problems. This allows your conscious mind to focus on things other than work. Your mind will be much more creative in generating new ideas that contribute to your organization's inventiveness. Some of the most creative breakthroughs have been made when people's minds were off duty or AWOL (absent without leave).

The average working person's life is out of balance. This is especially true in business, where many white-collar workers are working more than a regular forty-hour workweek. People regularly working excessive hours are workaholics. Perfectionism, compulsiveness, and obsessiveness are traits that complement the workaholic mentality. It is important to note that workaholics aren't peak performers: Workaholics are weak performers. The following chart points out the differences between workaholics and peak performers.

Workaholic	**Peak Performer**
➤ Works long hours	➤ Works regular hours
➤ Has no defined goals—works to be active	➤ Has defined goals—works towards a major objective
➤ Cannot delegate to others	➤ Delegates as much as possible
➤ No interests outside of work	➤ Many interests outside of work
➤ Misses vacations to work	➤ Takes and enjoys vacations
➤ Has shallow friendships developed at work	➤ Has deep friendships developed outside of work
➤ Always talks about work matters	➤ Minimizes talk about work matters
➤ Is always busy doing things	➤ Can enjoy "goofing off"
➤ Feels life is difficult	➤ Feels life is a celebration

Workaholics are addicted to continually putting in long hours and find no time for leisure. Considering the excessive work in which workaholics must indulge to get limited results, most are virtual incompetents. In fact, many workaholics end their careers by getting fired. Workaholism is a serious disease. If not treated in time, workaholism can result in mental and physical health problems. According to Barbara Killinger, author of the book *Workaholics: The Respectable Addicts,* workaholics are emotional cripples. The work obsession of workaholics leads them to ulcers, back problems, insomnia, depression, heart attacks, and in many cases an early death.

Because peak performers enjoy both work and play, they are more effective workers. When needed, they can turn on bursts of speed for a week or two. However, peak performers can be lazy (and proud of it) when the nature of the work is routine.

> Hard work is the soundest investment. It provides a neat security for your widow's next husband.
> —Unknown Wise Person

For peak performers, success in life isn't confined to the office. Being a peak performer with a balanced lifestyle means your job is serving you rather than you serving your job. Life/work planning consultants advocate a balanced lifestyle in which needs in six areas of life are satisfied. The six areas are: intellectual, physical, family, social, spiritual, and financial.

Figure 4-1. Balancing Your Wheel of Life

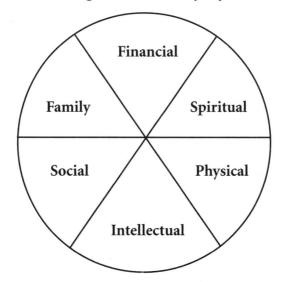

Since many companies have the philosophy that security, pay, and retirement benefits are the only way to motivate employees, your job may only adequately satisfy your needs in the financial and social areas. Your other four needs then have to be satisfied away from work.

Leisureholics Have More Fun

By working diligently (sometimes not so diligently) for forty years or more, many workers hope that one day they will cash in their chips for fifteen to twenty years of fruitful leisure. Upon reaching retirement, many people are unprepared for leisure, because they haven't indulged in much while they were working. Most people don't change until they have to change. They wait until retirement is a reality and then desperately try to make the adjustment. For the unprepared, the adjustment is extremely difficult because of the drastic change in circumstances. The time to start developing many interests and enjoying leisure is when one is working. A gradual adjustment is much easier to make. The following letter was written to me by Carrie Ollitac of Toronto.

> Dear Ernie,
>
> I just finished reading your wonderful book, *The Joy of Not Working.*
>
> I am a twenty-four-year-old workaholic, and I just wanted to let you know you have made me look at life in a whole new light! I am glad I was able to read your book so early in life so that I may begin to "live" so soon!
>
> Thank you
>
> Carrie Ollitac

This letter was one of the shortest I received, but its message is powerful. The corporate world would rather support workaholism at the expense of employees having balanced lifestyles. In organizations, workers are being rewarded for structured thinking and tunnel vision that supports the corporate mission. If leisure activities are encouraged, most organizations encourage activities related to work or those activities that will help employees perform their work better. Most organizations aren't interested in employees having many broad interests unrelated to work.

Also, many North Americans engage in leisure activities with little or no quality. The activities in which they engage are for the purpose of recuperating from a hectic day or week, not for the sheer enjoyment from the activity. Many activities aren't leisurely. Rather than relieving stress, the activities add to stress.

It is in your best interests, especially if you want to eventually live the Life of Riley, to have many interests unrelated to your career. Leisure isn't something to be saved up until you are totally without work. Living a balanced life means indulging in leisure throughout one's life.

If you are going to be addicted to anything, then be addicted to leisure—leisureholics have more fun than workaholics.

As a leisureholic, not only will you have more fun, you will prepare yourself beforehand for the time when you could lose your job. Spare time handled in a leisurely way, besides making you happier while working, prepares you for a better life when you find yourself unemployed. Retirement consultants suggest employees should start preparing and planning for their retirement when they are thirty-five years old or younger. Interests and new skills not cultivated before retirement are difficult to cultivate after retirement.

Helen Thomas, United Press International bureau chief at the White House for over twenty-five years, states that of all past presidents she knew—Johnson, Nixon, Carter, and Reagan—only Jimmy Carter truly accepted retirement and found it satisfying (quoted from the book *Are You Happy*, by Dennis Wholey). Jimmy Carter has been the most successful in retirement because his identity wasn't tied to the job and to having to be recognized all the time. Carter also had many ongoing interests—such as writing, working with wood, and building furniture—that he has actively pursued since leaving the presidency. The citizens of the United States appear to know Carter is the best off. In a recent poll, 45.1 percent of respondents named Carter as the living ex-president who conducted himself most effectively and appropriately since leaving office, while 18.5 percent chose Ronald Reagan and 9 percent chose Richard Nixon.

Figure 4-2. Before and After for a Workaholic

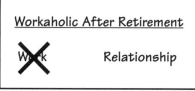

Workaholic Before Retirement	Workaholic After Retirement
Work Relationship	W~~or~~k Relationship

Figure 4-3. Before and After for a Leisureholic

Leisureholic Before Retirement	Leisureholic After Retirement
Work Relationship Golf Tennis Jogging Stamp Collecting Church Reading Gardening Volunteering Friends	W~~or~~k Relationship Golf Tennis Jogging Stamp Collecting Church Reading Gardening Volunteering Friends

Figure 4-2 shows the effect of losing a job when you have no interests. If you have only your job and a relationship (marriage or otherwise) to keep you busy, your life will be narrowly focused once you lose your job. Without a job, you are limited to your relationship for things to keep you active. Figure 4-3 shows the effect of losing your job if you have many interests and hobbies. As a leisureholic, you don't have to rely solely on your relationship for fulfillment, since you can shift your extra time to a range of activities and interests.

Breadth in interests is important. Life can feel empty if your interests aren't varied. While you are working, it is important to develop many eclectic interests outside of your career. Just one interest, such as golfing, will not be enough to fill your days. Ensure that you have a varied combination, from writing books to playing golf to visiting friends to taking a course unrelated to your job. It is also important that you choose activities that provide some purpose and achievement.

Leisure should be a quiet and enthusiastic absorption in things done for their own sakes and unconnected to work in any way. When you take time for leisure, try to adopt the European approach rather than the American approach. There is an important contrast in the philosophy of leisure in America and Europe. In North America, corporate philosophy tends to rule employees' lives, even in leisure. Because America has a working tradition rather than a leisure tradition, leisure to corporate America has been a time for relief and escape, to recharge one's batteries for the work ahead. In Europe, leisure is viewed in a different light. Leisure is for leisure's sake and not for work's sake. The main purpose of vacations is for enjoying leisure, not for recharging. Quality leisure in Europe is a result of a leisure-class tradition that has spanned many centuries.

After two weeks of vacation, you finally have a smile on your face.

I can't wait to get back in the office to tell everyone what a great time I had, even though I didn't.

For leisure to be effective during your career, it is best that you spend your spare time in a leisurely way and not in a competitive way. The spirit in which you conduct your leisure time may actually make this time more stressful than work itself. In North America, the traditional vacation is, more often than not, another tightly scheduled week with an itinerary resembling a week at the office. The week is spent at a spa or ashram retreat, with little or no choice for spontaneity. A ski holiday in the Rockies or the Alps is filled with so many activities that relaxation is nearly impossible. To add to the stresses, many vacationing employees keep in regular contact with the office. It is no wonder that the widely used Holmes and Rahe Social Readjustment Rating Scale for stress indicates people find vacations more stressful than they find the Christmas season, even though people experience quite a bit of stress before Christmas. Vacations would be much less stressful if people spent their time reading a book, getting to know the neighbors, or writing a novel just for the fun of it. More leisurely vacations are also better ways to prepare for retirement.

Few women and fewer men have enough character to be idle.
—E.V. Lucas

Another example of competitive leisure is one that I see at my tennis club. I go out and play tennis to get in shape and have fun. In contrast to this, many of the people on the tennis courts are even more competitive than they are in the corporate world. The looks on their faces indicate a level of seriousness normally reserved for funerals and wars. They will do anything to win: pick the most talented partners, choose inferior opponents, or cheat at the game. If they don't win, they will lie to a friend about the result of the match. To me, these aren't people enjoying leisure; these are people with serious problems.

Why You Should Be a Connoisseur of Leisure

Elizabeth Custer, private-time editor for *Glamour* magazine, recently telephoned me from New York to solicit my opinion on why the magazine's readers indicated in a survey that they are usually more exhausted on Sundays than they are on Fridays. Surprised by the survey's results, I had to give some thought to the question before I could give an adequate answer.

The answer lies in the Protestant work ethic. Someone visiting from another planet would think that most human beings must have serious kinks in their brains to utilize their leisure the way they do. Because of the Protestant work ethic, many people feel anxiety or guilt when they try to relax. Instead, they get busy doing things. Weekends are used to attend to miscellaneous chores and personal business. Time is spent on repairing houses, mowing lawns, and caring for children. Weekend busyness adds to the burnout already experienced during the workweek. Because of the self-imposed demands on their time, people are spending less time on the basics, such as sleeping and eating. It is no wonder that workers feel more exhausted on Sunday then they do on Friday.

Leisure is supposed to be easy for us to handle on weekends and when we retire. Nothing is further from the truth. We are socialized to work hard and to feel guilty about not working. Many people are afraid of free time, or just plainly don't know how to enjoy it. Some researchers say most Americans don't want more leisure time; they only get meaning and satisfaction from doing things.

Discipline and a certain attitude are required to utilize leisure time wisely. To be a connoisseur of leisure, you must regularly stop and smell the roses. Leisure should transcend just being a time to rest for the sake of one's work. True leisure time is spent at activities such as intimate conversation, tennis, sex, or watching a sunset; it is for the sake of enjoying the activity itself. True leisure is anything that is done for sheer pleasure, not so one can be more productive at work.

If you can't think of any leisure activities to enjoy, you are working too hard and haven't spent enough time getting to know yourself. It is never too late for you to develop a new interest or learn a new sport or skill. Having the ability to enjoy not working may come in handy at various times during your working years.

Four Important Reasons to Be a Connoisseur of Leisure

> ➤ If you go to a job interview desperate for the job, your desperation is likely to be noticed by job interviewers. Being happy without a job puts you in a much better frame of mind while you are job hunting. If you aren't desperate for a job, your positive attitude will show, and you will stand a much greater chance of being hired for the job.

> ➤ With high rates of unemployment here to stay, most people will experience more and longer periods of unemployment. Therefore, it only makes sense to learn to be as happy as we possibly can without a job.

> ➤ If you base your identity on your work, you lose yourself when you lose your job. When your identity is based on other elements, you have your identity with or without a job.

> ➤ If you learn how to be happy without a job, you won't be as afraid of losing your job when you get another one. You will be confident that you can still find life enjoyable, regardless of your situation.

To be leisurely, learn to take a rather unconventional approach to leisure. Don't be like the fast-trackers in the corporate world who engage in their leisure with as much, or more, competitiveness than they show at the workplace. They miss the whole point behind leisure. Take a vacation at home and refuse to keep in contact with the office. Treat yourself to an unexpected day off to add some spontaneity to your life. When in between jobs, take a vacation for a month or two. The goal is to be as leisurely as you can be. You will be more relaxed during your work life and more prepared for your retirement.

> The first half of life consists of the capacity to enjoy without the chance; the last half consists of the chance without the capacity.
> —Mark Twain

Many futurists are now predicting that work as we have known it since the industrial revolution is likely to be virtually phased out. As more robots and computers are used to replace human labor, less work will be available for the general population. The future will demand that you learn how to be a connoisseur of leisure.

Fire Yourself If Your Employer Doesn't

Work can create an imbalance in your life. Some jobs demand unending attention and won't give you the opportunity to have a balanced lifestyle. The result is often an unhappy spouse, undisciplined kids, no social life, and a miserable you. If you're getting about as much payoff from your job as being the captain of the *Titanic,* then you must do something to change your state in life.

> It's good to have money, and the things money can buy, but it's good, too, to check up once in a while and be sure you haven't lost the things money can't buy.
> —George Horace Lorimer

Here are some signals that your life is not in balance and you are probably in the wrong job:

- ➤ You take more than your share of mental-health days due to headaches, tension, and other stress-related complaints.
- ➤ You dread going to work practically every morning.
- ➤ You make field trips on the coldest days in winter, even though your job is an office job.
- ➤ You just don't like this job because you can't express your creative side.
- ➤ Your main interest in staying in this job is to cope for another sixteen years until you can collect a good pension.

> ➤ The first hour of work is spent reading the boring sections of yesterday's newspaper.
> ➤ You're married to your job; your life is all work and no play.
> ➤ You can't remember when you last got excited about your job.
> ➤ You have a hard time justifying your existence.
> ➤ Your job is undermining your health with problems of insomnia, excessive stress, and no time to relax.
> ➤ You daydream away over half of the work day.
> ➤ You keep trying, but to no avail, to convince yourself and others that your work is stimulating.
> ➤ You are just going through the motions.
> ➤ You have trouble concentrating and can't generate any new ideas for your projects and problems.
> ➤ You steal from your employer and try to justify it.
> ➤ What was once tolerable in your job now makes you angry.
> ➤ When you think about your workplace, you get depressed.
> ➤ You have lost all sense of commitment to your job.
> ➤ You long to be back in university or school, even though you didn't like attending either one.
> ➤ At 5:00 PM on Sunday afternoons, your stress level increases dramatically because Monday you have to go back to work.
> ➤ You have nothing good to say about your company, even though it recently made it to *The 100 Best Companies to Work for in America.*

We all have a tendency to grow comfortable with existing conditions, even those undesirable to us (there are many forms of mental illness). In the workplace, we end up tolerating dead-end jobs, professions we dislike, and companies that mistreat us. The workplace can also be a major source of boredom. A Lou Harris survey found 40 percent of Americans are bored sick with their jobs. We resist making changes because we fear the unknown. I was one of these people when I was last an engineer. Reluctant to quit, I stayed on until I was fired. In retrospect, I now realize that I subconsciously helped put on the shoe that kicked me out.

There is something wrong with my eyesight. I can't see going to work.
—Teddy Bergeron

The first day your job does not nourish and enthuse you is the day you should consider leaving. Fire yourself if your employer doesn't. Even if you generally like your job, if it takes more than fifty hours a week from your life and you aren't pleased with your unbalanced lifestyle, it is time for action. If your spouse calls you a stranger, your kids are on drugs, and you are miserable, why not do something else? My advice is that you **quit!** Forget about these excuses: I can't quit because I need the security, I need to make payments on my big house, I want to send the kids to college, and all the other excuses that arise. Don't wait for the right time to quit. Do it now because there is never a right time; waiting for the right time is another convenient excuse to justify procrastination.

Regardless of how much money you earn, you will never be able to recover the forty hours or more you are putting into a job that doesn't enliven you. It is impossible to buy back enough enjoyment in retirement to make up for the pleasure you missed while working at a lousy job. Ask yourself, "What good is the money going to do if I lose my health?" Many rich people can't buy their health back.

> All paid jobs absorb and degrade the mind.
> —Aristotle

Many people work with the same company until retirement, even if they don't like their job or the company, because they don't want to give up their good salaries. Others, like two schoolteachers I know, hate what they are doing, but won't change careers because of the generous retirement benefits. Staying in an unpleasant job or undesirable career makes these people function at much less than an optimum level. It also increases their chances for experiencing burnout before retirement, so they won't get to enjoy the retirement benefits.

You are imprisoned by the system if you are working just for the money. Don't allow society's idea of financial security to dictate your life. Spending time at a job you hate just to make money will interfere with your ability to enjoy life. As odd as it seems, it will also interfere with your ability to make money. There is a common feeling that getting one's financial state in order will help put the individual's other needs in place. The opposite is frequently true. Studies have confirmed that individuals who do what they like generally end up making much more money than individuals who work in jobs they dislike, just for the money. It is important to be growing in your job, doing what you like, and putting your favorite talents to use. Attitude jumps back into the picture. If you feel your work is valuable and enjoyable, chances are you will attract enough money to enjoy life.

> Work is the greatest thing in the world, so we should always save some of it for tomorrow.
> —Don Herold

It's not impossible to leave a job, just difficult. Don't fool yourself by thinking something is impossible when it is only hard. If you want to do something, and are committed to doing it, you can do it. There is a price to pay, but it will be worth it in the long run. Do your wife a favor, do your kids a favor, do your organization a favor, and do yourself a favor. If you are a schoolteacher, college instructor, or university professor who dislikes your job, also do society a favor by quitting, since you have no business teaching in the classroom.

If you are considering quitting your job, ask yourself, "What is the worst thing that can happen if I quit my job?" Then, after pinpointing the worst thing that can happen, ask yourself, "So what?" If the downside doesn't involve death or terminal illness, then say the heck with it all. It's not the end of the world. Put things in proper perspective; focus on the positive rather than the negative, and life changes dramatically. First of all, you have your health, and you are alive. Now think about all the options in your life. In North America, even without a job, you have more opportunity than millions of people can ever dream about having on this earth. As for worrying about security, there is no such thing as true security from holding on to a job. Knowing you have the ability and creativity to always make a living is the best financial security you can have.

Think about the great activities in which you can participate between this job and the next one you undertake. You can sell everything you own and take the money and travel around the world. You can go to China and Rio and Mexico. You can go to Spain and paint. You can write the book that you always dreamed of writing. You can sleep in until ten o'clock. Of course, when it's time to go back to work, you may wind up with a much better job than you had before. Once you fire yourself, you may not want another job if you can somehow avoid one without incurring severe financial hardships. Many people feel better about themselves when they quit corporate life. Even those people who don't find something financially rewarding say they would have a hard time returning to their old corporation.

There will always be some risk in leaving your job; everything worthwhile carries some risk. Besides, you may get fired sooner or later anyway. Remember, with downsizing so prevalent in the 1990s, the odds are increasing that your company will set you free, whether you like it or not (a good sign that this is about to happen is when you are given a secretary who is illiterate). By voluntarily leaving your job, you get to handle being without a job. You will be more proficient at handling the tough situation when it surfaces again.

> Learn to pause ... or nothing worthwhile will catch up to you.
> —Doug King

Before the update for this edition, several people wrote to me to happily inform me that they quit their jobs after reading *The Joy of Not Working*. The material on the previous pages was instrumental in helping people, such as Les from London, to leave their jobs. Following is the complete content of Les's letter.

Dear Ernie:

I have just finished reading your book *The Joy of Not Working*. Your inspirational words have changed the way I now view my life. I always felt that working harder would eliminate my problems, but all it ever did was complicate my life and cause more problems. You have given me the courage to quit my job. I used to be a tax consultant. Now I'm a human being again.

That's right. I marched in this morning and told them I quit because my wife, my kids, and my health (both mental and physical) were more important. I've been seeking security through working more but that's not the answer. There are so many things I've wanted to do but felt I couldn't. I love reading, and I've always felt writing would be a natural extension of my personality. If you have the time, I'd appreciate learning how you got started writing. I also failed first-year university English.

Thank You,

Les

The greatest risk may be in **not** leaving your job, as it apparently was for Les. He has written to me twice since his original letter, and he was doing just fine the last time I heard from him. If you cannot risk being fully alive, what can you risk? Going through the motions in your job means you spend eight to ten hours a day in a boring, joyless, and lackluster way. When your job is taking its toll on your spirit, body, and mind, it is time to get out, whether or not you have another job. There are some things you shouldn't sacrifice for any job. Your dignity and personal worth must come first. If your freedom is at stake, get out of the job immediately. No job is worth it if the personal sacrifices you have to make will interfere with your enjoyment of life to the fullest.

Are You Listening to Your Calling?

One of the chief sources of happiness for successful individuals is having a special purpose or personal mission. If you are having a hard time getting out of bed in the mornings, you haven't found your personal mission. Having an important purpose in life means being truly alive. In the mornings, if you have a purpose, you can't contain your high level of excitement and enthusiasm for the day ahead. You can't wait to get started, whether it is raining, snowing, or sunny outside. Your personal mission is a calling in life that comes from your soul; it is your essence and reason for being. Your personal mission is why you came into this world.

The reason so many people from the baby-boomer generation are suffering from midlife crises is they never pursued their passions. During the 1980s, most of these people pursued careers or jobs that paid the most money, so they could live the yuppie lifestyle of excessive materialism. They may have achieved career success as they defined the term: getting to the top of the corporate ladder and collecting material possessions. But their marriages may be in shambles, their children all messed up, and they themselves may be suffering from excessive stress and dissatisfaction.

> The deepest personal defeat suffered by human beings is constituted by the difference between what one was capable of becoming and what one has in fact become.
> —Ashley Montagu

Happiness is finding your personal mission and responding to it with passion. It is important to find your personal mission if you are to live life with an overarching purpose. Most unhappy people haven't found their ultimate purpose or personal mission. Many haven't found it because they haven't searched for it; some haven't found it because they don't know how to find it.

Your life will be much more rewarding if you put in the time and effort to find your personal mission and then pursue it with passion. Neglecting your ultimate purpose or personal mission will cause you much dissatisfaction. Avoiding what you love may result in emotional turmoil and physical ailments. People who suppress their true interests and desires are most likely to get addicted to alcohol, drugs, work, or television in a futile attempt to ease the pain and dissatisfaction in their lives.

> It is not enough to be busy ... the question is: what are we busy about?
> —Henry David Thoreau

A personal mission is on a higher level than a goal. A goal, such as becoming general manager of your organization, leaves you nothing to live for once you reach it. A personal mission, such as making the world a better place to live by having everyone reduce their pollution, is a higher calling. You can pursue this all your life.

> Every calling is great when greatly pursued.
> —Oliver Wendell Holmes, Jr.

Everyone can discover a primary purpose for living. Your personal mission can be expressed through your career or avocation, but it doesn't have to necessarily involve your work. It can also be expressed through volunteer work, a pastime, a hobby, or some other leisure activity. Your ultimate calling in life can be expressed through a combination of the various facets of your life, including your interests, your meaningful relationships, your work, and your leisure activities.

The *Vancouver Sun* recently reported on Vancouver nun Sister Beth Ann Dillon, who expresses her mission through basketball, her favorite sport. Needless to say, her personal mission is serving God by serving others. She lives a simple life, free of material trappings, but one of joy. Basketball adds to her joy and helps her fulfill her mission. It seems Sister Dillon has loved basketball as long as she has loved God. Through her volunteer work, she teaches basketball to girls in an elementary school. She believes playing basketball can bring people closer to God. In 1989, she met Pope John Paul in Chicago; she has also met Mother Teresa. Now that Vancouver has its own team—the Grizzlies—in the National Basketball Association, she is excited about the possibility of meeting Michael Jordan.

I sometimes lie here meditating a bit about my greater purpose in life, but most of the time I just fantasize about what I will do when I win a million dollars in a lottery.

Deepak Chopra, in his book *The Seven Spiritual Laws of Success,* gives seven laws for achieving success effortlessly. His seventh law is "dharma," which means one's duty, unique talents, and important purpose in life. You won't lack zest for life if you discover your personal mission. Your essential nature will determine your purpose and what you truly want to accomplish in your life.

Your personal mission has nothing to do with making money. Having a personal mission or purpose means utilizing your unique talents in such a way that the conditions for humanity are enhanced. Your life is also enhanced because of the satisfaction and happiness you experience. While utilizing your talents in pursuing your mission, several by-products may result; one by-product may be making a lot of money.

A musician must make music, an artist must paint, a poet must write, if he is to be ultimately at peace with himself.
—Abraham Maslow

A personal mission will be closely tied to your values and interests. It will also be determined by your strengths and weaknesses. A job that you take for the sole purpose of making money or a leisure activity in which you participate to kill time is not a personal mission. Your personal mission is something that will make a difference in this world. If you have an overarching purpose in life, you know that humanity is benefiting from your efforts. A mission can be modest by other people's standards. For example, a friend's father is a school janitor whose mission is to create the cleanest school possible for the students and teachers. Here are some other examples of personal missions:

Music is my mistress and she plays second fiddle to no one.
—Duke Ellington

> ➤ To make the world a better place to live by reducing pollution
> ➤ To raise money to help care for others in need
> ➤ To help children develop a special talent or skill such as playing a piano
> ➤ To write entertaining children's books that help young boys and girls discover the wonder of the world
> ➤ To give foreign travelers the best possible tour of the Rocky Mountains
> ➤ To create a committed relationship and keep it exciting and energizing

Your personal mission will intimately connect you to who you are and to the world around you. Taking the time to answer the following questions may help reveal a personal mission that you would like to pursue.

1. **What are all your passions?** Discovering what turns you on is the most important element for recognizing your personal mission. Your passions give you great enjoyment; you seem to have unlimited energy when pursuing your passions. Write down all the things you find enjoyable. Your list can include things as varied as fishing, horses, serving others, researching at the library, making people laugh, and traveling to other countries. Pay attention to the things that would get you out of bed an hour or two earlier than your usual time.

I never thought of achievement. I just did what came along for me to do—the thing that gave me the most pleasure.
—Eleanor Roosevelt

2. **What are your strengths?** Looking at your strengths says something about yourself and where you like to concentrate your energy. If you are artistic and able to go with the flow, you may

want to create art or music or sculpture. Strengths normally support passions.

3. **Who are your heroes?** Spend some time thinking about your hero or heroes who would be good role models. Heroes can be people from the past or present you have admired, or even revered. They can be famous or obscure people who are doing something special or outstanding. If you were given the opportunity, which three role models would you choose to have dinner with? What have these people accomplished that you admire? Studying your heroes' qualities and actions will give you clues about your own aspirations.

> The purpose of life is not to be happy. It is to be useful, to be honorable, to be compassionate, to have it make some difference that you have lived and lived well.
> —Ralph Waldo Emerson

4. **What do you want to discover or learn?** It is important to look at what stimulates your curiosity. Which topic or area would you like to explore more? Think about the courses or seminars you would select if a wealthy relative appeared out of nowhere and offered to finance two years of study anywhere in the world.

Answering these questions may put you on the right track to discovering your personal mission. When you get in touch with your innermost desires, you are connecting with your personal mission. No one else but you can discover your ultimate purpose in life.

The Secure Workplace Is a Fool's Paradise

The 1961 musical *How to Succeed in Business Without Really Trying*, a parody of corporate life in America, was revived in March 1995 on Broadway. The play suggests that anyone who wants to attain career success should ingratiate oneself with the boss, pick the right work team, and stab the right backs. To succeed, it is necessary to be a yes-man or yes-woman to the right people. Also imperative is selecting a corporation so big that nobody knows exactly what anyone else is doing—a large government department will also suffice. Although corporate memos have little use to anyone, to succeed you must read and write a lot of them to expose your name as much as possible. Success will depend more on avoiding risks than on intelligence and actual work output.

Is this you today? Are you looking for job security with a large company or a government department that guarantees long-term employment until your retirement in exchange for your loyalty and dedication? You may expect that your employer, during the course of your career, will notice how valuable you are due to your ability to write memos and be a yes-person. You may also expect to be well-rewarded financially and promoted many times.

If these are your expectations, some management consultants say you are a fool in the company of many other fools. According to these management consultants, surprisingly, many people—young and old—still have these expectations. The expectations of a secure full-time job and the opportunity to climb the corporate ladder were encouraged by the majority of educators, parents, and by society until recently. Having these expectations today means you have lost touch with reality and replaced it with a good fantasy.

Today, the secure workplace is a fool's paradise. The traditional workplace has been shrinking for the last few years; the secure job has now gone the way of the dinosaur. Don't blame anyone but yourself for having these false expectations. Cradle-to-grave employment with one company has been a fantasy for several years and won't return during your lifetime, if ever again.

Don't be like so many people today who are still looking to corporations for a safe place to hang out. Contrary to what many people believe, the world without job security isn't a case of doom and gloom. Ultimately, you are the one who has to handle a world without job security, or at least change the concept of job security as we presently define it. No employer can be the guarantor of job security as we used to know it.

Your first loyalty should be to yourself. This may sound selfish, but it is no more selfish than the employer who wants your loyalty for the company's gain. Your notion of job security will have to be redefined if you are to succeed. Job security must be defined as your knowing that you have the courage to handle any situation. You have to be the source of your job security; your creativity and resourcefulness will mean that you survive.

Having Your Cake and Eating It Too

If you would like to keep working at your present job or career, but at the same time want a more leisurely lifestyle, you are in the group of individuals who want to have their cake and eat it too. Here is some good news: Contrary to popular belief, you can have your cake and eat it too. It's really quite simple; just get yourself two cakes. See! You are already ahead of all those workaholics and competitive fast-trackers, because they wouldn't ever think of this.

Although few people in the fast lanes of corporate America achieve optimal leisure, you can, if you put your mind to it. If you want to have a balanced lifestyle, first you must learn how to be a peak performer by working fewer hours. As stated in Chapter 3, some of the greatest achievers in the history of humankind have been creative loafers. Peak performers get ahead by slowing down. They aren't always busy, because they know how to loaf. To be a peak performer, work smarter, not harder. How this can be accomplished in a job is beyond the scope of this book, but there are some excellent books devoted to this topic.

Based on some studies of available leisure time for the average worker, it appears a rigid career track offers little opportunity to properly enjoy and handle leisure. One such study—a 1988 Louis Harris poll—indicates the average American workweek jumped from under forty-one hours to almost forty-seven hours between 1973 and 1988. Leisure time shrank 37 percent. This means less time for hobbies, vacations, and just plain loafing.

Other studies contradict these findings. One study indicates that, because of fewer children and less housework, the majority of North Americans have more free time—about five hours—now than in the recent past. The problem, according to these studies, is not one of insufficient leisure. Instead, most people underestimate the amount of leisure time they have available and don't use it constructively. Generally, North Americans have about forty hours a week of free time. Behavioral studies show free time is available, but most North Americans waste it. About 40 percent of their free time is used watching television. Much of the other time is spent taking care of such things as cooking, cleaning, shopping for groceries, repairing the house, paying the bills, and doing work taken home from the office. It's simply a case of undertaking too much. As a result, most working Americans feel less rested on Sunday than they do on Friday.

Despite what the studies say, I am not convinced that the average American or Canadian has no control over the decrease in his or her leisure time. If you haven't enough time to catch a breath of air, let alone smell the roses, it's probably because you are to blame. Practically everything in your life is a matter of choice. The lack of leisure time is mostly self-imposed; anyone who has too little time has simply undertaken too much work or collected too many material possessions.

To have a better balance, you must get to work relaxing. Making time for leisure should be a priority. Many of the solutions are quite basic. One is simply to leave the office at 4:30 or 5:00. You will have more energy to pursue other interests. In doing so, you will show you are an interesting, competent person and one of the real leaders of the 1990s. Also learn to undertake fewer tasks at home. Spend less time shopping, cooking, cleaning, and repairing the house. Many of us allow these things to take up too much of our time.

Conventional approaches to work arrangements prevalent in the 1970s and 1980s do not provide us with the best opportunities for optimal leisure and satisfying lifestyles. Progressive organizations realize that a well-balanced lifestyle means blending leisure and work. Leisure should be enjoyed when the employee wants it, and should not be reserved for weekends, vacations, or retirement. Here are some programs for enhancing employees' lifestyles that are gaining popularity in the 1990s:

➤ Sabbaticals (paid or unpaid) for all employees
➤ Phased retirement to gradually increase leisure
➤ Telecommuting to reduce travel time
➤ Flextime for flexible leisure and to reduce travel time
➤ Job banks
➤ Banked overtime, which is used for paid time off
➤ Job-sharing to reduce work hours
➤ Part-time jobs to reduce work hours

These alternate work options are ways to improve the quality of your leisure time. Finding companies that support these programs may be difficult, but more and more companies are receptive to these new programs. If your company isn't thinking of adopting any of these options, it's time to start looking for a new employer. There are other things you can do if you really want to have more leisure: Switching jobs or careers can open up possibilities for more leisure. Living closer to work and reducing commuting time is another option.

A balanced lifestyle means having at least one quarter of non-sleeping time unscheduled. Otherwise you aren't winning at life. Allow generous amounts of time for yourself to get to know and develop yourself. It is a mistake to put aside sports, travel, and active pursuits because of a spouse, children, job, and a need to earn a living. You can always squeeze in leisure activities if they're worth it. Just in terms of health alone, you cannot afford to discount creative loafing from your life. Having fun in your personal life will carry over into your work; your job will be more enjoyable because you are more relaxed.

I would not exchange my leisure hours for all the wealth in the world.
—Comte de Mirabeau

The most important point of this chapter is that you should be pursuing your leisure interests now. You may have to perform a remarkable balancing act to get a more balanced lifestyle, juggling your career, your debts, your possessions, and even your children. If you have a job that doesn't allow you to do this, then you should find yourself another job. Whatever you have to do, do it. Life is too short to devote to voluntary slavery.

If you are going to work, you should put emphasis on blending a lifetime of work and leisure into a well-balanced lifestyle. A balanced lifestyle with a satisfying career and many fulfilling non-work-related activities involves having your cake and eating it too. Having the cake and eating it too isn't for everyone— only for those people in charge of their lives.

The Joy of Not Working Nine to Five

In 1982, Ben Kerr was successful according to society's definition of success. Then, he quit his job as an assistant credit manager with the Toronto Harbor Commission after an office reorganization left him sitting beside a man who smoked cigarettes. Kerr couldn't stand the smoke, and when higher management didn't respond to his concerns, he quit. Since then, he hasn't worked for anyone else. He is now a busker at the intersection of Yonge and Bloor in Toronto.

When I met Ben, the first thing I noticed is that he is an extremely happy man. While he sings his songs throughout the afternoon, people from all walks of life continually say hello to him and give him money. Inspired by this book, Ben has written a song called "The Joy of Not Working Nine to Five." Here are the words to the song.

The Joy of Not Working Nine to Five

I know the joy of not working nine to five
Singing every day at Yonge and Bloor
Strumming my old five-string guitar
It's the joy of not working and that's for sure

People say that I'm a lucky guy
And they wish that they could be like me
To know that joy of not working from nine to five
To be foot-loose and fancy-free

But they'll never lose the treadmill that they're on
And it's sad to see dejection in their eyes
The joy of not working could be there
But they're just too afraid to try

Ernie J. Zelinski wrote a book
The Joy of Not Working is its name
'Cause Ernie is a fellow just like me
And the joy of not working is his game

I know the joy of not working nine to five
Singing every day at Yonge and Bloor
Strumming my old five-string guitar
It's the joy of not working and that's for sure
The joy of not working and that's for sure

© 1994 by Ben Kerr

Ben has been offered jobs, but he isn't interested in working for someone else. He is having too much fun. He gets more satisfaction from singing at Yonge and Bloor than most people get from their work.

If you have recently been downsized, or are about to be, it may be a blessing in disguise. Now may be the time to challenge your need for security and your unwillingness to take a risk. Searching for a regular job may appear to be the safe way out, but you may be selling yourself short. You may actually attain much more security by pursuing a career with your personal mission in mind. And if you really enjoy your work, you will never have to "work" another day in your life.

CHAPTER 5

Unemployed: The True Test of Who You Really Are

The Time of Your Life to Have the Time of Your Life

The intent of this chapter is to help you make an easy and comfortable transition to more leisure in your life. Many years of preparation are normally put into entering the world of work, but little or no preparation is usually undertaken for leaving it. The time of your life to have the time of your life is when you are retired or temporarily unemployed. Without work, you will discover a whole new and exciting world out there. Being away from work allows you to enjoy life in a way not available to you when you are working. Not having to work creates the ideal time to enjoy leisure time, a time like you never had before.

> To be able to fill leisure intelligently is the best product of civilization.
> —Bertrand Russell

The day you wind up with a great deal of spare time, through retirement or unemployment, is the day you get to test who you really are. Extra leisure time will be a gift from heaven, if you have taken the time to grow as a person and if you haven't tied all your identity to your job. Learning to enjoy being unemployed involves the ability to experience everything through your own essence, instead of through the demands and directions of society, the business world, and the media.

It is just as important for you to handle spare time when you are temporarily unemployed, as when you are permanently retired. Career specialists say the general outlook is that people will have to rebuild their careers several times in a lifetime. The average time spent on one job is now only 3.6 years. Employees will be more vulnerable to firings and layoffs than ever before; no job is safe anymore. The average forty-year-old white-collar worker can expect to change employers three times in his or her career, with at least one firing or layoff. If you are in between jobs at this time, make the most of it. Handling joblessness will make you more confident in handling it again when it happens in the future, including when you retire.

This time like all times, is a very good one, if we but know what to do with it.
—Ralph Waldo Emerson

Your attitude and degree of motivation will determine how well you utilize extra spare time. The transition to more leisure is not always an easy one. While you are working hard and trying to get rich and famous, you aren't learning how to handle leisure. You are learning how to work hard, and how to try to become rich and famous. These skills are not easily forgotten. Even when you have the opportunity to relax and enjoy life, you may have a difficult time breaking away from your habit of working hard.

Writing a New Script for Your Life

Virtually everyone who loses a job because of retirement or unemployment is affected in some significant way. Those who say they aren't are either crazy or lying. Being fired, laid off, or retired is initially hard to handle for most people. As I found out, it isn't quite as easy as shooting fish in a barrel or rolling off a log.

How much one has identified with one's job is a factor in how much difficulty one will experience away from a job. The greatest loss of identity accompanying the loss of a job is experienced by people who have totally immersed themselves in their work. For those who have totally tied their identities to their jobs, grieving the loss may take some time. Managers and executives normally experience a harder time during unemployment and retirement than blue-collar workers, because white-collar workers identify more with what they do.

Most of us have relied on outside forces, such as the business media, universities, and corporations, to provide a script for leading what society considers a successful life. Most of society's institutions haven't written into their script a way for people to handle a life of total leisure. All of us will need to put effort into writing a new script for leading worthwhile and satisfying lives when we experience a dramatic increase in leisure time.

Although people nearing retirement have a fear of diminished purpose and activity, sooner or later, most of them successfully make the transition to a life of leisure. Unfortunately, some people have been so rigidly socialized with unworkable Puritan values that they find being without a job difficult, distasteful, and depressing. Because of their unhealthy attitudes and unwillingness to change, rigid individuals experience a serious loss of self-esteem, as demonstrated by the suicide rate for American men, which is four times higher in retirement than in any stage in life.

People who claim it is extremely difficult or impossible for them to have a worthwhile life without work are saying they have no individuality. They are, for all intents and purposes, admitting that their personalities are extremely shallow, and their basis for existence is entirely externally oriented.

> A stiff attitude is one of the phenomena of rigor mortis.
> —Henry S. Haskins

I will assume you aren't so rigidly socialized that there isn't any hope for you; this is a safe assumption since rigid people don't normally read books like this. In addition, I will assume you can write a new script for your life that will help you make the transition to more leisure. If you have strongly identified with your job, don't expect instant breakthroughs. Allow the process to take time, since you will be remaking your self-image. You may initially feel like a loser, but this will change as your self-image improves. Your money-making goals have to be replaced with leisure-oriented goals. What you must do is to start getting some sense of accomplishment out of your leisure activities. Over a period of time, your self-image will change to that of a winner.

Rediscovering Your True Essence

With the end of a job or career comes the end of a source of identity. If there is no new job or career to replace the old, leisure must provide the means to meet human needs that the job met before. In making the transition to a life of total leisure, a person will find the first few days or weeks the most difficult. Some people can experience fright and panic; others feel the situation is unnatural.

An important element in making a transition to more leisure is the discovery of your true essence. If you have been totally obsessed and absorbed by your work, you may have had little in the way of the leisurely life. In fact, you may barely have had a life—period.

Your career may have provided you with most of your identity. You may have allowed your career, over the years, through the demands and nature of your job, to transform yourself. What is dear to your company, instead of what is dear to you, may have become ingrained. Careers have a nasty habit of eroding our essence, our true self.

Rediscovering your essence—what is important to yourself—can take a little time. It will take some digging around—mainly within yourself—to find out what makes you tick. You will have to show commitment, by using your ability to grow and learn, in this new situation. Once you have discovered your true essence, you won't require the trappings of a job to define who you are.

> There are two things to aim at in life: first, to get what you want; and, after that, to enjoy it. Only the wisest of mankind achieve the second.
>
> —L.P. Smith

Evidence indicates that with time most people adjust to being without a job and find life to be as satisfying, or even more satisfying than with a job. Morris M. Schnore, a former professor of psychology at the University of Western Ontario, conducted an extensive research study on the well-being of retired people. His findings, stated in his book *Retirement: Bane or Blessing,* support the notion that people don't need a job for happiness and satisfaction in life.

After leaving work, a majority of people have discovered their true essence and found retirement to be fulfilling. Only a small minority suffers from a prolonged identity crisis. Schnore found that for a small group—10 percent—retirement causes a serious maladjustment. People with negative attitudes towards retirement place work in a central position in their lives.

Schnore concluded that satisfaction in life was commonly found to be as high, or higher, among older adults as among younger adults. He discovered that, contrary to the negative myths about retirement, retirees were happier and more satisfied with their lives than middle-aged workers. Almost half the retirees—43 percent—stated that their health had improved with retirement. Some retirees found retirement was better than they expected. According to Schnore, several factors contribute to effective adjustment to retirement:

➤ Striving for goals that are attainable

➤ Developing an appreciation for what one has

➤ Confidence that one can cope with problems as they arise

If you are making a transition to more spare time, there are going to be many changes in your life. As you shift from work to more leisure in your life, you can't help but recreate your true essence. You will find there is no reason to feel incompetent or worthless because you don't have a job. Once you find the inherent value in leisure, you should have little trouble coming up with new ways to keep yourself challenged—with or without help from someone else.

A New Paradigm for Success

If you have always felt uneasy and guilty about enjoying activities unrelated to work, you will require nothing short of a paradigm shift to master the extra spare time that accompanies joblessness. A paradigm is a belief or explanation of some situation that a group of people share. A shift from an old paradigm to a new paradigm creates a distinctive, new way of thinking about old problems. Normally a new paradigm involves a principle that was present all the time, but overlooked.

Your paradigm shift must involve a change of your beliefs about the nature of leisure. First and foremost, you must think of leisure as a worthwhile pursuit—as worthwhile as any job you ever had. A life of total leisure doesn't have to be frivolous and unfocused. Leisure doesn't equate with a lonely life filled with boring daytime soap operas and reruns of *The Simpsons,* although this is what it winds up as for unmotivated people who hang on to old beliefs. The realm of leisure can mean much success in your life.

Success is getting what you want; happiness is wanting what you get.
—Unknown Wise Person

The feeling of success is just as attainable without a job as it is with a job. The success peddled by society means a good job, a big home, and a luxury car. This isn't the only way to define success; success can be defined in many ways. When a person has a paradigm shift, success takes on a different meaning. I like Ralph Waldo Emerson's definition of success:

What Is Success?

To laugh often and love much;
To win the respect of intelligent persons and the affection of children;
To earn the approval of honest critics and endure the
betrayal of false friends;
To appreciate beauty;
To find the best in others;
To give of one's self without the slightest thought of return;
To leave the world a bit better, whether by a healthy child, a rescued
soul, a garden patch or a redeemed social condition;
To have played and laughed with enthusiasm and sung with exaltation;
To know that even one life has breathed easier because you have lived;
This is to have succeeded.

—Ralph Waldo Emerson

Notice that all of Emerson's definition of success is possible away from the workplace. Joblessness doesn't have to mean being unproductive or being a loser. You are a loser only if you see yourself as one. As mentioned in Chapter 2, perception is everything. You will have to change your perception of yourself if you see yourself as being unproductive without a job. You can see yourself as a winner because you are privileged to have so much leisure to engage in the productive pursuit of self-actualization. Not many people in the history of this world have had this opportunity.

Remember that the great philosophers, such as Plato and Aristotle, adopted the right attitude in early Greece. The pursuit of leisure wasn't looked upon as laziness or uselessness. Total leisure led to greater self-knowledge, which was the highest purpose in life. Anyone who attained the state of leisure was definitely highly privileged to be able to practice self-actualization. You should adopt a sense of privilege at the opportunities a life of leisure makes available to you.

Reminiscing about Great Jobs That Weren't

The key to being happy to have left your last job is to overcome whatever nostalgia you may experience about that job. When we think about something from the past, often we think about the good things and forget the bad. I know some people who even reminisce about things that never happened. With jobs, we remember the things we liked and forget all the things we disliked. Often we tend to miss the good old days that never were.

Let me share how I have been able to overcome nostalgia for former jobs. About four years ago, I still had some difficulty in making the transition from a sixteen-hour-a-week instructor's job to no job at all. Despite the enjoyment that I had received from many extended periods of total leisure and the fact that this job only took sixteen hours a week, my transition to more leisure wasn't as easy as I had anticipated. In the mornings, I was raring to go, but there was just one slight problem: I had no place to go. I started missing the things that my last job offered, or so I thought.

For the first two or three days, I had misgivings about having resigned from this job. Nevertheless, around the fourth day, I was back in the groove. The feeling of prosperity returned. I started feeling sorry for people who had to go to jobs that they didn't like. I even felt sorry for those who liked their jobs. They couldn't possibly be enjoying themselves as much as I was enjoying myself.

> As lousy as things are now, tomorrow they will be somebody's good old days.
> —Gerald Barzan

One way I handled leaving this job was by thinking about the things I disliked about working in that organization, as well as other organizations in which I worked. This quickly put my unemployment in proper perspective. Whatever nostalgia I had was quickly put to rest.

Exercise 5-1. Telling the Truth About Your Last Job

Think about the most recent job you left. List the things you didn't like about your boss, the organization, or the daily events associated with going to work.

> Nostalgia isn't what it used to be.
> —Unknown Wise Person

Based on the organization where I had the sixteen-hour-a-week job and other organizations at which I have worked, I made my own list of the things I disliked about having to work at the typical workplace. Here are twenty-five good reasons for feeling fortunate to be without a regular job.

Twenty-Five Reasons to Dislike the Typical Workplace

- ➤ An excessive workload as a result of corporate downsizing
- ➤ Being confined in the office all day when the sun is shining

- No opportunity for advancement for at least fifteen years because the baby boomers holding senior positions are not moving anywhere
- Having to work with jerks and incompetents who should have been fired ten years ago
- Power struggles within the office involving fierce competition, backstabbing, and paste-on smiles
- Receiving less pay than someone who is much less productive but who has been around longer
- Commuting for an hour or two each way, every day, in the jungle of traffic
- Being restricted to a desk all day—unnatural inactivity
- Constant interruptions and no time to think because of the daily pressure
- Paperwork—memos that mean nothing and reports no one ever really reads
- No cooperation from other departments
- Double-talk, or even triple-talk, by superiors
- Regular two-hour, or longer, meetings that go nowhere fast
- Having to work with repulsive workaholics who refuse to take vacations even when they are encouraged to do so by the employer
- Too rigid vacation schedules that make it impossible to take vacations at the best times of the year (the months that don't have an "r")
- The organization asking employees not to take full vacation entitlements because of too much work
- Supervisors taking credit for others' work and ideas
- Lack of good parking for employees (except for overpaid executives)
- Having to stay the full workday even if you are twice as productive as someone else and get your work done ahead of schedule
- Bureaucracy, red tape, foolish rules, illogical procedures, and unmotivated people specializing in dynamic inaction
- Discrimination due to race, sex, physical features, or being single
- Organizations that advertise themselves as being innovative but don't support innovative people
- Office air-conditioning that functions properly only in winter

> ➤ No recognition or acknowledgment for excellence in work
> ➤ Working with repulsive yes-men and yes-women who prostitute themselves for salary increases and promotions

Since the above situations are par for the course in most North American organizations, it's no wonder many people consider the workplace demeaning to the human spirit. If you miss your old workplace, think about all the above situations with which you had to deal. If your old workplace had most of these situations, and you still miss it, quite frankly, you have a lot of problems. Put down this book now and make your next destination a psychiatrist—before it's too late. Hopefully, he or she will be able to help you.

Reading the above list from time to time should put things in proper perspective and bring a smile to your face in no time if you aren't working. If you are working, any smile you may have had will probably quickly disappear after reading this list.

Three Needs to Satisfy at Your Leisure

Most of us don't tell the truth about the workplaces we leave. After we leave a job, we don't necessarily miss the work; we miss the things the job brought with it. Although most people don't realize this, a job is more than a means for getting an income. A job satisfies many other needs besides money. Especially if we have a supervisory or management position, the job provides us with many rewards: self-worth, status, achievement, recognition, room for growth, and power. Upon leaving the job, these rewards are lost. Leisure will be satisfying only if it can provide most of the rewards we find important. All our needs, which were previously satisfied at the workplace, will now have to be met in different ways.

There are three important human needs that most jobs inadvertently fill. The needs are structure, purpose, and a sense of community. Even if we work at a job that is not highly desirable, the modern-day workplace provides us with the means for satisfying all these three needs. Once we leave the workplace, all these needs have to be met from our leisure.

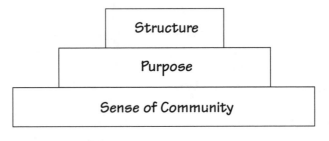

Three Important Needs

1. Erecting New Structures

Structure is set by society from the time we are children until we retire. Tasks, such as getting an education, working at a job, getting married, and raising a family, all have ready-made structures associated with them. The problem arises when we find ourselves away from the workplace, with substantial free time on our hands. Upon our retirement or job loss, the structure we had in our jobs disappears abruptly. Now we have to design our own structure. We have to rearrange our lives, which requires some effort.

Initially, the loss of ready-made structures and routines sounds great: no need to get up early in the morning, no need to rush breakfast, no meetings to attend on time, and no commuting in rush hour traffic. In other words, the clock no longer rules us. The problem is that most of us, no matter how creative we are, like at least some structure and routine in our lives. Being creatures of habit, we get addicted to structure. There is a great deal of comfort from the routines. Of course, we all like comfort.

Having to lose structure and routine can create much havoc, especially for very rigid and highly structured people. Time must be filled to pass the days, but empty time can end up being the rule instead of the exception. Empty time results in boredom and joyless living. Rigid people may even withdraw from society and lead a life of desperation because they refuse to adjust to an existence in which they have the personal freedom to do what they want. In extreme cases, mental and physical capabilities rapidly deteriorate.

If you are independent, creative, and motivated, the loss of structure will be a blessing rather than a curse. This is the time to enjoy your freedom and to create your own new structures in your life. Structure can be established in many ways. For example, I had to create my own structure and routines when I gave up the ready-made structures provided by the organizations where I worked. Exercising twice a day to keep fit puts routine and structure in my days. I do stretch exercises for about fifty minutes first thing in the morning. In the late afternoon, I exercise for another one and a half hours by cycling, jogging, or playing tennis. Besides all the other great benefits I get from exercising, I get two and a half hours of routine every day. I also put more structure in my days with activities such as regularly visiting my favorite local bistro to have coffee, chat with the regulars, and read three different newspapers. Setting regular time slots to write this book, as well as two others, has provided me with even more structure.

I'm trying to arrange my life so I don't even have to be present.
—Unknown Wise Person

Motivated people erect their own structures to replace those that existed in a former job. Self-made structures and routines can be established with the multitude of activities available in the world of leisure. Below are just a few ways to put routine and structure back in your life:

> ➤ Take courses at your local college or university.
> ➤ Jingle your car keys at four o'clock each afternoon.
> ➤ Join the boards of charities that meet regularly.
> ➤ Involve yourself in a sport, such as tennis, golf, hockey, or soccer, which you can do on a regular basis.
> ➤ Work as a volunteer.

When you lose old structures, you must build new ones. No one will do it for you; I certainly won't (I have too many coffee bars to visit). How you deliberately develop your routines and structures is up to you. If you have developed as a person, your interests should be so varied that the lack of routine and structure won't be a problem. The task of setting some routine and structure will be much easier if you have set some goals and created some driving purpose in your life.

2. Being on Purpose

Many hardworking men and women know how to get things done in the workplace, but find themselves lost once they gain more freedom. With the loss of a job, the self-worth these people previously extracted from being productive and attaining goals is shattered. Their purpose is set out for them at work and disappears when they lose their jobs. These people have never taken the time to explore themselves and find out what they want to do in pursuit of a higher purpose.

Having a purpose when one is unemployed can be a matter of life or death. People without purpose don't seem to live as long as those with purpose. Statistics indicate that retired people without a purpose in their lives aren't known for breaking many records for longevity. Seven in ten people die within two years; the average receives only thirteen Social Security checks before checking out of this world for good. It appears that these people, who have been addicted to work, lose their purpose and self-worth once they lose their jobs. If they had established some other purpose in their lives, the purpose could have been the driving force in retirement that would have added many years to their lives.

If you are retired, your work may have been important to you. It may have been a great creative outlet; however, you can make leisure as important. Many activities can provide a creative outlet. Purpose doesn't only have to come from a job where someone else creates your purpose. Without a job, a sense of productivity and achievement is still possible, but has to come from other sources.

Don't feel bad about being unemployed, Dad. I've been unemployed my whole life and it's fun!

When I was fired over ten years ago, my purpose for the next two years was enjoying my life without working at a job or attending an educational institution. I developed a passion for leisure and ended up with a sense of accomplishment, even though many capable and intelligent people would have gone bonkers under the same circumstances. I could lay claim to going two years without a job and enjoying practically every minute. Because I didn't have the distractions of work and other events during those two years after I was fired, I learned more about the world and myself than I did at any other time in my life.

You must learn to focus on your purpose or lack of purpose. Discovering your purpose is the cornerstone for using your creativity. The biggest challenge will be looking within, discovering your purpose, and living out that purpose. A good way to find your purpose is to fill in the blanks to these self-discovery statements:

To change the world I would like to_____.

Wouldn't it be great if I could _____.

Someone with purpose whom I admire is _____.

At the age of 95 I would like to look back and say this is what I have accomplished: _____.

I would get satisfaction in my life if I could _____.

All successful people, whether at work or play, have found a purpose for their being. Here are some of the ways people have found purpose in leisure time:

- ➤ To make a difference in people's lives
- ➤ To make a contribution—i.e., community work
- ➤ To find creative expression
- ➤ To take part in discovery and challenge
- ➤ To help preserve the environment
- ➤ To show other people how to enjoy life
- ➤ To accomplish or achieve some challenging task
- ➤ To improve health and well-being
- ➤ To create personal happiness and satisfaction

Meaning can be found in many leisure activities. You can establish an educational mission or a helping-other-people mission or a self-actualization mission. With an overriding purpose, you will have more energy than you can use. You will be under less stress, and your life will be in greater balance.

The key is to create a purpose for which you have a passion. If you can establish some ultimate goal or mission in your life, you will have a fiery driving force to keep your life exciting and interesting. This will ensure you are constantly growing and learning; your life of leisure will never be without purpose. Your purpose should relate to your essence and your dreams. Being on purpose means each task, act, and situation will be worthy of your total attention.

The secret of success is constancy of purpose.
—Benjamin Disraeli

3. Generating a Sense of Community

Beyond business, accomplishment, and power, the office has become a community center. The office is not only where workers make a living. Unlike in the past, the office is also where friends are made and after-work activities are arranged. An important component of happiness for people is a feeling that they are making a contribution to a community. Jobs provide the feeling that individuals are appreciated, valued, and cared for by co-workers. For some employees, the need to be loved is also fulfilled at work.

I don't care to belong to any club that will accept me as a member.
—Groucho Marx

For many people, the workplace is the only source of social involvement. A sense of belonging is provided in work groups, teams, committees, departments, and after-work activities. Work also provides the means for contacts that we require for socialization. The majority of working people make most of their new friendships in the workplace. If we have been receiving socialization forty hours a week from our work for thirty-five or forty years, it isn't easy to lose all this contact. With the loss of the job, we also lose our best opportunity to make new friends.

Most of us also require some support systems for psychological and emotional health. For most working people, these are mainly provided by the workplace. When they lose their jobs, these support systems disappear.

If you have lost the socialization and support systems you had at work, you can't wait around to be discovered. The way to regain the opportunity for socialization is to get involved in new groups, associations, and organizations. Look to colleagues, friends, neighbors, family, clubs, charitable organizations, and community leagues as a means of getting more community in your life.

Don't stay away from church because there are so many hypocrites. There's always room for one more.
—Unknown Wise Person

What groups you join obviously depends on your needs and interests, but the important thing is to take at least two or more nights a week to go out of your home and into the world around you. Try to get involved with a group—large or small—that has a defined purpose. The organization you get involved with can be community oriented, or it can be related to church, hobbies, or current affairs. In this way, you can establish new social bonds. Furthermore, you establish a purpose and create the opportunity to attain recognition.

While you are out socializing, keep in mind that learning from others is an effective way of gaining wisdom in life. Find someone who is having a ball away from the workplace. Notice what they do. It simply makes good sense to seek the company of those who are good at handling leisure and living life to the fullest. You will see they create their own purpose, structure, and sense of community.

Making a Career Out of Leisure

The day you wind up retired or temporarily unemployed is the day you have to look at leisure as a career. The rewards from this new career are satisfaction, self-actualization, and achievement of meaningful goals. You shouldn't feel worthless because you don't have a job. Look at yourself as making an incredible contribution to society by being able to handle being without a job.

The concept of making a career of leisure will go against many of your friends' or acquaintances' instilled values. Ignore any negative comments directed at you because someone feels you aren't making a contribution to society when you aren't in the workforce. These comments come from mediocre or small minds. Think of the sources of these comments as totally irrelevant or insignificant to your life.

If people still aren't satisfied with your contribution to the world, let them know how much more motivated you have to be at what you do than at what they do. It takes very little ingenuity and motivation to go to a job where a structure and purpose are laid out for them by someone else. There is really a lot less challenge in going to a structured job and a set routine, than in handling a life of leisure where you have to create your own structure and purpose. You must be a lot more motivated to plan your own days with constructive activities than to respond to something other people have created for you.

During my lengthy periods of not working, people have often asked me what I do for a living. I have replied, "Nothing. At this time I am too prosperous to work. I am presently a connoisseur of leisure."

When someone has persisted and asked me if I am financially independent, I have countered with my ace-in-the-hole reply: "I was talking about being mentally (and not financially) too prosperous to work. It is most unfortunate you haven't progressed to this state of mental prosperity, but I am sure with a lot of work you can get there." This normally shuts the person up

Great spirits have always encountered violent opposition from mediocre minds.

—Albert Einstein

and leaves the person in a state of confusion. This is the way I like to see anyone who is so narrow-minded that they think everyone's career should entail working for a living.

Recently, I received the following letter from Karen in Toronto:

Dear Ernie:

I have just finished reading your book, *The Joy of Not Working*, for a second time and felt compelled to write a letter of thanks.

This past July I quit a job that was both frustrating and extremely stressful. It was taking a toll on my health. At that time I saw you on CBC-TV and read your book. Everything that I had been feeling for quite some time was in the book. It was so refreshing to know that someone else viewed the world of work the same way as myself.

For six wonderful months I have lived the Life of Riley that has been both exciting and relaxing. I had the chance to travel to Eastern Canada and to Thailand, as well as reading a ton of books and magazines. I got to know my family and friends again. And most importantly, I got to know myself. Of course, others were extremely envious of my position—which actually equates to FREEDOM.

Unfortunately, I am not in the financial situation to live independent of a regular full-time job. Alas, I have obtained a new job and will start this January. The important change has been in my attitude, in that I now realize it's okay not to be a workaholic, and I am determined to again live the Life of Riley (semiretirement at least).

Sincerely yours,

Karen Hall

Note that Karen is a connoisseur of leisure. To her, being without a job is a privilege. More leisure time should make you feel privileged rather than anxious. If you can discover your true essence, there can be great substance to your life away from a job. A healthy attitude ensures you will hold on to your personal worth and dignity. Without the confines of the workplace, you gain certain freedoms: freedom to think, freedom to reflect, and freedom to act. Your time can be filled with infinite possibilities. Remember, being without a job is the true test of who you really are—and truly an opportunity to become who you want to be.

CHAPTER 6

Somebody Is Boring Me; I Think It Is Me

An Extremely Boring Disease to Have

Two gentlemen of leisure, a North American and a European, were discussing the joys of life when the European nonchalantly stated that he knew a hundred different ways to make love. The North American, somewhat in awe of what he had just heard, replied that he knew only one. The European asked which one it was. The North American described the most natural and conventional way. The European then replied to the North American: "Most interesting, I never would have thought of that! Thanks a million. Now I know 101 ways."

> He was known for ignorance; for he had only one idea, and that was wrong.
>
> —Benjamin Disraeli

Are you like the North American or the European? Do you see only one way of doing things, or do you look for many? The habit of looking for one way, and the most conventional one at that, will set you up for the disease described in the following exercise.

Exercise 6-1. Don't Get This Disease

This disease afflicts over 20 million North Americans. It can give you a headache or a backache. It can give you insomnia or make you impotent. It has been labeled as a cause of gambling, overeating, and hypochondria. What is this ailment?

If you, at this moment, have a headache, are reading this book because you can't sleep, and are deeply craving a giant five-decker sandwich after having just eaten one, you are probably bored. The ailment described above is none other than boredom.

Now recognized as one of North America's most serious health problems, boredom is at the root of many psychological disorders and physical problems. Some of the common physical symptoms of boredom are shortness of breath, headaches, excessive sleeping, skin rashes, dizziness, menstrual problems, and sexual dysfunction.

Boredom deprives people of the meaning of life and undermines their zest for living. Although it would seem to specifically affect those who are idle and jobless, people in the workplace can be just as affected.

People who are chronically bored have certain characteristics; they are:

➤ Anxious for security and material things

➤ Highly sensitive to criticism

➤ Conformists

➤ Worriers

➤ Lacking in self-confidence

➤ Uncreative

At work or at play, boredom is most likely to hit people who choose the safer, no-risk path. Because they take no risks, bored people seldom reap the payoffs of accomplishment, contentment, and satisfaction.

People who choose the path of variety and stimulation are rarely stricken with the ailment of boredom. To creative individuals, who look for many things to do and many ways of doing them, life is tremendously exciting and fun. Just ask the European who now knows 101 ways to make love, if you ever run into him.

How to Be Really Boring to Other People

Boring people are victims of their own behavior. Unfortunately, everyone they associate with also falls victim to their "boring" behavior. If the most exciting thing that happened in your life is that you know someone who met John Grisham at a book signing, then you may be a touch boring.

Some people are so boring that they make you waste an entire day in five minutes.

—Jules Renard

People who complain about themselves and utter trivialities are more boring than people who overuse slang or try too hard to be nice, suggests an article in the November 1988 issue of *Personality and Social Psychology*. Researchers, Mark Leary, assistant psychology professor at Wake Forest University, and Harry Reis, psychology professor at the University of Rochester in New York, went so far as to establish a boredom index to determine which behaviors were deemed more boring than others. The following are behaviors cited in Leary's and Reis's study:

- ➤ Overusing small talk or slang
- ➤ Complaining about oneself
- ➤ Trying to be nice to be liked by others
- ➤ Showing no interest in others
- ➤ Trying to be funny to impress others
- ➤ Going off on tangents
- ➤ Talking about trivial or superficial things

Boredom flourishes too, when you feel safe. It's a symptom of security.

—Eugène Ionesco

Make sure that you adopt all of the above if you want to be really boring to other people. All of the above behaviors tend to bore most people. Some of these behaviors are more boring than others. Reis and Leary found that the most boring behaviors were talking about trivial or superficial things and showing no interest in others. The least boring behaviors were trying to be nice and trying to be funny.

We are all boring sometimes, and most of us are interesting sometimes. Some people are more boring than others. The question is how boring are we to others? If we are boring to others, we are probably boring to ourselves.

You may be undermining your opportunities for enjoyment of leisure involving social contact if you conduct yourself in ways that are boring or questionable to others. Here are some traits and behaviors some people may consider boring.

> ➤ Your idea of quality time is spending an hour or two talking to your horse and drinking a few cans of no-name beer.

> ➤ You have more than one picture or statue of Jesse Helms or Newt Gingrich in your living room.

>> ➤ Your idea of luxury accommodation is sleeping in the back seat of an abandoned Mercedes-Benz.

>> ➤ You can't figure out why someone who is strong, big, and husky is a member of a men's support group.

Plato is a bore.
—Friedrich Nietzsche

>> ➤ You belong to a fitness club where half of the members own pit bulls, and the other half wish they did.

> ➤ You love your car, your stereo, your dog, or your pet snake more than you could ever love a marriage partner.

> ➤ Your idea of a wild Saturday night is taking a ride on the bus and then hanging around the laundromat for a while.

> ➤ Your favorite T-shirt says: "I like sex, watching TV, and drinking beer."

> ➤ You drive around with more than one flat tire.

> ➤ You have been divorced three times and you are only twenty-five.

> ➤ Regardless of which of your three sweaters you wear, someone is always saying something like "How long do you have to wear that sweater before you win the bet?"

> ➤ Your idea of a gourmet meal is a TV dinner with two or three cans of no-name beer.

> ➤ You brag about how well-educated you are because you took three years of grade nine.

Your image may suffer if any of the above statements describe you. Whether you are boring will depend on how many people say you

Do you think I'm boring?

I know we've met, but who the heck are you?

are. Here is a good way to tell whether you are what someone says you are. If you encounter twenty people in a day, and one calls you a horse, don't worry about it. If you encounter twenty people in a day, and two people call you a horse, you still don't have too much about which to be concerned. However, if you encounter twenty people in a day, and seventeen or more call you a horse, then you should immediately get yourself a saddle and start eating hay! Of course, the other alternative is to stop being a horse.

If you have negative charisma, and you are the life of the party only when you leave, you must do something about your personality. You must pay the price needed to correct the deficiencies. Psychologists confirm that charismatic people aren't born with their charisma. The special charm that attracts others like a magnet and energizes them can be learned. What you must do is develop an inner radiance and project a love of life when you are with people. Charisma is displayed when you have high self-esteem; it reflects itself in your high positive energy and joie de vivre.

The Real Cause of Boredom

To a certain degree, we all get bored some time in life. Ironic as it may be, many of the things we strive for can end up boring us: A new job, in time, becomes boring. An exciting relationship can become dull. Leisure time once deemed as precious may become dead time.

When we get bored, there are many things to blame: society, our friends, our relatives, low-quality TV programs, uninteresting cities, a depressed economy, the neighbor's stupid dog, or a gloomy day. Putting the blame on external forces is the easiest way to react; this way we don't have to take responsibility.

Psychologists report that certain factors contribute to boredom. Some of the most common causes of boredom psychologists cite are:

> ➤ Unfulfilled expectations
> ➤ Unchallenging jobs
> ➤ Lack of physical activity
> ➤ Being too much of a spectator
> ➤ Seldom being a participant

In order to live free and happily, you must sacrifice boredom. It is not always an easy sacrifice.
—Richard Bach

A good question arises: Who is responsible for our lack of physical activity, unfulfilled expectations, being in unchallenging jobs, or being a spectator instead of a participant? We only end up being bored if we allow these things to manifest themselves in our lives.

Of course, we are the ultimate authors of our boredom. We must make our lives more interesting, if that is what we want. Placing blame on people, things, or events seldom, if ever, solves our problems. No one else can solve our problems for ourselves. Eliminating boredom is dependent upon the willingness to take responsibility and do something about it. When we take the steps to avoid being bored, boredom is no longer a problem.

Dylan Thomas said, "Somebody is boring me, I think it is me." If you are ever experiencing boredom, remember who caused it; you and only you caused it. If you are bored, it is because you are boring.

The Easy Rule of Life

People afflicted with boredom take the no-risk route because it is the most comfortable. All of us have the tendency to seek comfort at some time or other. In fact, most of us take the comfortable way all the time. The problem with choosing the comfortable way is it turns out to be very uncomfortable in the long run. This is best explained by what I call the "Easy Rule of Life."

Figure 6-1

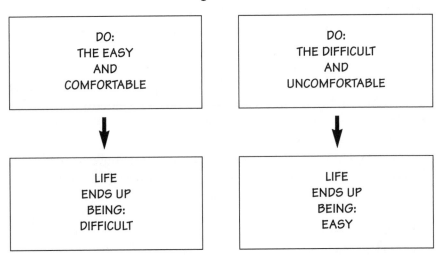

Figure 6-1 represents this rule. What the Easy Rule of Life dictates is that when we choose the easy and comfortable route, life turns out to be difficult. Ninety percent of us choose this route because short-term comfort seems more appealing than the alternative. The other option is to take the difficult and uncomfortable route. When we choose the difficult and uncomfortable route, life is easy. Ten percent of us take this route because we know we must experience short-term discomfort for long-term gains.

The biggest obstacle to success is the discomfort in doing the necessary things we must do to attain success. As human beings we gravitate toward less pain and more pleasure. Choosing the easy way ensures we wind up in a rut. And the only difference between a rut and a grave is the dimensions. In the rut you get to join the living dead, and in the grave you get to join the dead dead.

Let me warn you that The Easy Rule of Life is something like the law of gravity. Mess around with the law of gravity by walking off the top of a building and see what happens to you. It knocks you on your butt. The same thing applies with the Easy Rule of Life. Mess around with it by taking the easy way and you wind up on your butt as well. It seems to work every time.

Everything in life has a price. Leisure with a difference requires effort. Most people take the course of inaction because at the time it seems the easiest. In the end they cheat themselves out of the big payoffs. Take my advice and don't be one of the majority who chooses comfort at the expense of accomplishment and satisfaction.

The Easy Rule of Life had a bit of an influence on Lynn Tillon from New York. She sent me the following letter after she read the first edition of this book:

Dear Ernie

In the last few minutes I've followed some of your suggestions from *The Joy of Not Working.*

1) Wanting to write to you—and actually doing it

2) Doing the "difficult" now so that life will be easy

3) Breaking the rules of writing to a "stranger"—only using a business-letter form

4) Writing a letter—which I haven't done in ages (though constantly promising myself that I will)

Unlike some, I could put the book down—because I wanted to savor the information, be ready to do the exercises—and at other times couldn't. The words pulled me along—addictively. Last night *The Joy of Not Working* kept me awake for hours—forcing me to think, plan, and figure out what I really want to do with my life. Then finally, this morning, it was finished. And while I was thinking that writing to you would be great, I saw the page with your address.

I teach juvenile delinquents in a NYS Division for Youth Facility. I made copies of the easy rule of life. The kids were interested and enthused and came up with parallels in their own lives that amazed me; e.g., easy money selling drugs leads to family pain, danger, death, jail. If I had tried to bring these things up, it would have been preachy.

Personally, I want **out** of the job and the lifestyle of driving over three hours a day—leaving little precious time for leisure—to say nothing of the stress. Your book has given me hope and many tools to free myself for living, and also to enjoy the present more until I decide to change.

I'd love to hear from you. I will let you know how well I am progressing in my plan to get out of my job.

Sincerely,

Lynn Tillon

Handling People Who Would Even Bore a Saint

We all have a boring acquaintance or two who seem to know everything there is to know about what is boring. These individuals can be just a little unpleasant and difficult to be around. If you are like me, after a few moments with them you begin to squirm in your seat and look for some means of rapid escape.

There are more bores around than when I was a boy.
—Fred Allen

To eliminate the boredom of being with these people, you must take responsibility. First, you must get one thing straight: It isn't the boring person who is responsible for your boredom; it's you.

One alternative for dealing with boring people is to find some way of changing your perception about those you perceive as boring. Your voice of judgment may be to blame. Often we expect too much from other people and don't give credit where credit is due. To help yourself overcome your boredom with other people, practice being a saint. Look for something interesting and exciting about them. You may find that the boring person isn't so boring.

You may be thinking that this first alternative is okay for most people, but you know that one extremely boring person who will put anyone's saintliness to the ultimate test. In this case, you have to simply take the necessary action to minimize your time around that person. In the extreme case, you may even have to eliminate him or her from your life completely. In the end, it is up to you.

If You Do Boring Work All Day, You Will End Up Boring

If you look at truly happy individuals who are caught up in life, you will notice they are caught up in their life's purpose. Often their purpose is their work; however, their purpose can also be associated with a leisure activity or a passion. Many happy people with a zest for life have an overwhelming passion for their work. If you are working, is your work working for you? If it is, your work is your passion and constitutes part of your important purpose in life. Your important purpose will be manifested through your avocation when you are using your talents and creativity to make a difference in this world.

Clyde, you're boring me to death. I'm putting you on hold for a while.

Similarly, if you are not working because of unemployment or retirement, is your leisure working for you? If you participate in boring and monotonous leisure activities, you are likely to end up boring and monotonous. You must get involved in active leisure activities that contribute to more challenge and risk in your life.

If you are working and your job is primarily composed of tasks that you consider extremely boring, you should consider making changes in your job or leaving your job. Bob Black, in his essay "Abolish Work: Workers of the World, Relax," offers some important food for thought. He states: "You are what you do. If you do boring, stupid, monotonous work, chances are you'll end up boring, stupid, and monotonous."

I had a boring office job. I cleaned the windows in the envelopes.

—Rita Rudner

If you are stuck in your career, leaving a less-than-mediocre job won't be easy. You may need the money and not have time to look for another job. However, if you have some opportunity to leave a boring and dehumanizing job, you must do it now for your long-term health and happiness. Making too many compromises to your lifestyle for the sake of your job makes for a bored (and possibly a boring) you.

You Don't Have to Be Rich to Enjoy a Sabbatical

Although the two- or three-week vacation is adequate for taking a small rest, it often isn't enough to avoid boredom and burnout at a job. Becoming stale in your profession is something you want to avoid. If you are doing essentially the same thing you were doing three or five years ago, consider taking a sabbatical. No matter how hard you try to rest during three consecutive weeks of vacation, you won't get close to ridding yourself of the staleness. A well-rested and fresh mind is best attained through a decent sabbatical.

Seriously consider taking a sabbatical, so you can surround yourself with different people and look at the world with a new pair of eyes. If you haven't taken more than a three-week vacation for years, now is the time to experience a different world.

All work and no play makes Jack a dull boy—and Jill a wealthy widow.

—Evan Esar

In a fast-track world, the sabbatical is something everyone should try to take every five to ten years. This is a time to rejuvenate the body and soul so one can stay fresh in one's career. A leave of absence from work is a time to rejuvenate the spirit. A six-month sabbatical should be the absolute minimum. A two- to three-year sabbatical can be used to acquire a new degree, learn a new skill, or develop a new talent.

Richard Procter of Toronto sent me this letter in the summer of 1995:

Dear Ernie,

About a year ago, I somehow managed to win a door prize at the office I was working at, even though I did not show up for the party! I thought that was rather odd, but accepted the twenty-five-dollar voucher from a bookstore nevertheless. I browsed around a bit, and finally the title of your book caught my attention, so I grabbed it.

Well, you might be interested to know that your book did **not** change my life. It did, however, crystallize and confirm many of the principles I have been living by for years. You've managed to put and present in an excellent manner the many good ideas I've been mulling over in my head ever since I was faced with the prospect of earning a living, some twenty years ago now.

I work as a computer software consultant. These days I do short- to medium-term contracts. This method of work, followed by one to several months of inter-contract time off, allows me to pursue many of the leisure ideas your book covers, and a few that it doesn't. I can't imagine living any other way. I'm grateful that the computer revolution came along and gave me the opportunity to carry on like this! Travel is my main hobby. I just returned from two months in Mexico and S.W. United States, but I do lots of other stuff that nobody else seems to have the time for.

Anyway, I'm planning to visit Edmonton this summer around August 24th before I make a canoe trip on the Nahanii River. If you have the time, I'd be pleased to buy you lunch or dinner and have a chat about work and leisure. Let me know if this is convenient.

Thanks for writing such a good book.

Richard Procter

Because I was working on another book, I didn't reply to Richard until he had left Toronto for Edmonton. However, synchronicity struck again. While I was sitting with a friend at one of my favorite coffee places in Edmonton, Richard happened to be walking by with his cousin Nancy and recognized me from the picture of me on the back of the book. Richard and Nancy ended up buying me dinner a few days later.

To be a nobody, do nothing.
—B. C. Forbes

I found out Richard is a connoisseur of leisure. Richard has found that less is more; less work means more time for leisure pursuits. For Richard, a sabbatical at least once a year is a great way to enjoy life to the fullest. Boredom has no place in Richard's life. I last heard from Richard just before I undertook the revision of this book. He was on one of his sabbaticals in the Middle East with a former girlfriend from Australia; he wrote to me from Egypt.

Note that the sabbatical isn't only for the rich. Although I haven't made a great deal of money over the years, I have only had to work half of my adult life. The other half has been spent going to university or taking sabbaticals of various kinds. Be creative in designing a lifestyle with few material wants, and you will increase your ability to afford to take a sabbatical. Your freshness may propel you to make a lot more money than if you didn't take sabbaticals.

Boy Are You Lucky You Have Problems

Unwillingness to welcome and solve problems can add to boredom in our lives. Creative people look at most complex problems as opportunities for growth. We should all welcome problems in our lives as more opportunity to attain satisfaction from solving them.

How do you view day-to-day problems? Do you always look at a big or complicated problem as an unpleasant situation? Well, you shouldn't. The point is: the bigger the problem, the greater the challenge; the greater the challenge, the more satisfaction experienced from solving the problem.

There is no such thing as a problem without a gift for you in its hands. You seek problems because you need their gifts.
—Richard Bach

Being creative means welcoming problems as opportunities for attaining greater satisfaction. The next time you encounter a big problem, be conscious of your reactions. If you are self-confident, you will feel good because you have another opportunity to test your creativity. If you feel anxious, remember that you, like everyone else, have the ability to be creative and solve problems. Any problem at hand is a great opportunity to generate innovative solutions.

Many things have been said about problems and how we should handle them. The reality of problems can appear to range from the good to the bad to the ugly. Here are some points to think about. Whether the points are perceived as good, bad, or ugly will depend upon your interpretation.

You may dream of a problem-free life; however, it isn't worth living. If you were hooked up to a machine that did everything for you, all of your problems would be eliminated. It is unlikely you would find this an attractive substitute to life with its inherent problems. Remember this when you dream of a problem-free life.

If you want to get rid of your problem, just get yourself a bigger problem. Suppose you have a problem deciding what to do this afternoon. As you are contemplating your problem, a big, mean grizzly bear starts chasing you. The small problem of not knowing what to do in the afternoon will have been eliminated by the bigger problem of the grizzly. The next time you have a problem, create a bigger one; the smaller problem will disappear.

Solving a problem often creates more problems. This has many variations: Our problem may be that we aren't married. Once we get married, we then get to enjoy the problems of marriage. Another problem may be a lack of enough clothes. Once this problem is solved, we don't have enough closet space and don't know what to wear. Poverty, when solved with a lottery win, leads to many other problems, such as friends not having anything to do with us.

Major problems involving painful incidents or major personal setbacks are often opportunities for creative growth and transformation.

Many individuals report that going through a divorce or losing the whole wad in Las Vegas can give the mind a good rattling. The result is an experience of creative awakening.

Setbacks such as not being promoted at a job can result in a rebirth of creative thinking that had remained dormant for ages. Many people report that getting fired from a job was the best thing that ever happened to them. As indicated before, I am one of these people. Because of my major problem of being fired, I was given the opportunity to discover what I really wanted to do in life. Major problems are mind shakers that break old habits of thinking.

Putting Your Boredom at Risk

The last section stressed that problems are opportunities. The bigger the problem to solve, the greater will be the satisfaction from solving that problem. If this is the case, why do many people avoid problems more than they would avoid a pit bull terrier with rabies? One of the biggest reasons is the fear of failure when attempting to solve problems. The best way for us to get rid of our boredom is to take some risks in our lives. By subjecting ourselves to the chance of failure, we put our boredom at risk.

> In order to get to the fruit of the tree, you have to go out on a limb.
> —Shirley MacLaine

Moe Roseb put his boredom at risk. After purchasing my first book, Moe called me from San Diego to talk about the power of creativity. In our conversation we discussed the whole idea of taking risks in life. At forty-six years old, with the children gone, Moe decided to take a risk and move from Toronto to California. He talked about how his friends, many of whom he had known for years, were rather boring. Some were having midlife crises. Friends still saw Moe and his wife as being the same as they were fifteen years ago, even though both of them had continued to grow and develop as individuals. Moe felt that his relationships with these friends had stagnated.

So did Moe continue to blame his friends for his situation? No. He put his boredom at risk and did something about it. He moved to California to new friends, new surroundings, and a new life. Moe looked at it in this way: "Many of my friends are having midlife crises. I am going to have a midlife adventure instead."

Only Fools Are Afraid to Be Fools

On one hand, people in North America are obsessed with attaining success. On the other hand, most people are afraid of failure and try to avoid it. The need for success and the desire to avoid failure are contradictory. Failure is just a necessary step to success. Most of the time you will have to experience many failures before you experience success. The road to success looks something like this:

Failure Failure Failure Failure Failure **Success**

The road to most success is paved with failure—failure and nothing else. Yet many people attempt to avoid failure at all costs. The fear of failure is associated with other fears: the fear of being seen as a fool, the fear of being criticized, the fear of losing the respect of the group, and the fear of losing financial security. Avoiding failure means avoiding success.

If you want to double your success rate, just double your failure rate.

—Tom Watson

Many of us avoid risks because of our fear of looking bad if we fail. We get so obsessed with being liked that we won't do things which we feel may make us look bad in the eyes of others. Avoidance of risk becomes the norm. This can be very detrimental to our creativity and to our aliveness. We must learn to be fools if we are to be creative and live life to the fullest.

If you are reluctant to fail due to your fear of what people will think about you, I have news for you: Most people are going to think bad thoughts about you anyway. In fact, when you are successful, they will even find nastier things to say. The more successful you are, the more criticism you will attract. Most people's thinking about others involves criticism. It doesn't matter whether you are successful or not; you are going to be criticized either way. So, what's the big deal about failing? You may as well go for it! Chances are you will eliminate boredom and make a big difference in your life.

Figure 6-2. Fool's Chart

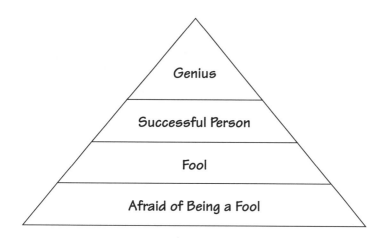

The Fool's Chart in Figure 6-2 emphasizes that being afraid of being a fool is on a much lower level than actually being a fool. Geniuses and successful individuals, whether at work or at play, have handled the fear of being a fool. They realize that in order to succeed in their endeavors, they must experience a great deal of failure and regularly risk being a fool.

Being foolish is essential to life's mastery. Being "a fool" will put you on a much higher plane of personal growth than will being "afraid of being a fool." Success in life requires that you be a fool now and then.

Dare to Be Different

Being creative at leisure is being able to think and do something unusual. In this way you can generate something new and worthwhile in your life. This will take courage since you will be criticized and frowned upon for having the nerve to stand out in the crowd. If you have a healthy attitude, you will be able to ignore the criticism or look at it as being totally irrelevant.

Making a difference in your life and in others' lives is a sure way to eliminate boredom. Keep in mind that you can't expect to be a conformist and still make a big difference. To make a big difference in this world, you have to start off by being different. Do something out of the ordinary and forget about what others think.

Albert Einstein, Thomas Edison, Mother Teresa, Mahatma Gandhi, and John F. Kennedy all made a big difference in this world. They all had something in common: They all were different from the majority of people. They were out of step with society; none of these great individuals were conformists.

Don't be a carbon copy; instead be an original. Take the time to think about how you are limiting yourself in your life by trying to be like everyone else. If you have an unhealthy need to always fit in and be accepted by everyone, you are setting yourself up for a life of boredom.

I would rather sit on a pumpkin, and have it all to myself, than be crowded on a velvet cushion.
—Henry David Thoreau

In addition, chances are others will find you rather boring. In other words, if you want your life to be boring, then conform and be dull; if you want your life to be interesting and exciting, then be different.

Boredom is something you experience in your life because you invite it in. The best way to overcome your boredom is to do something about it. Remember, if you are bored, it is because you are boring. The only person who can help you overcome this is yourself. You have the creative ability to make life exciting; use that ability. That's an order!

CHAPTER 7

Lighting the Fire Rather than Being Warmed by It

Dancing the Motivation Dance

Many years ago a young man mustered enough courage to ask a young woman to dance. After he had danced with her for a few minutes, the woman told him that he was a lousy dancer. She complained that he danced like a truck driver.

To many people, this experience would have been enough for them to quit dancing for good. Watching television or sitting around being bored would have seemed like much better alternatives. Nevertheless, this man developed a passion for dancing and continued to dance for many years after.

The young man continued dancing because he had the self-esteem and motivation to continue. He became known as one of the great dancers in modern times. At the time of his death in March of 1991, he had 500 dance schools named after him. At one time, he had been on television for eleven years straight, showing many different people—including truck drivers—how to dance.

> I could dance with you till the cows come home. On second thought I'd rather dance with the cows till you come home.
> —Groucho Marx

By now you undoubtedly know I am talking about Arthur Murray. He became great at his occupation because he was self-motivated. Aware of his own ability to learn and grow, he discovered his true potential.

The Arthur Murray story underscores the importance of attitude and motivation. Attitude and motivation go hand in hand. Only when you are self-motivated can you hope to accomplish the things that you want to accomplish. If you want to create a satisfying life of leisure, you must be able to dance the motivation dance.

Are You Motivated Enough to Read This?

You are reading this book because you motivated yourself to do so. The inducement could have been one of many: You were bored and had absolutely nothing else to do; you like reading books that stimulate your thinking; you are a masochist and like reading books you dislike; you read books like this one to put yourself to sleep; or you feel obligated to read this book because I bought you dinner last week. Whatever your reason, there had to be an inducement for you to pick up this book and read this far.

Motivated Tennis Player

Motivation is the act or process of generating an inducement or incentive for action. A lack of motivation will mean no action, and needless to say, nothing can be accomplished without at least some action.

It is generally agreed that unhealthy attitudes and the lack of motivation are major stumbling blocks to achieving success and satisfaction from adult pursuits. Although skill and knowledge are important, they don't guarantee success. Skill and knowledge only contribute about 15 percent to what it takes to be successful. At least 85 percent of success is attributed to having a high level of self-motivation and a healthy attitude.

According to David C. McClelland, a researcher on achievement and motivation, only 10 percent of the U.S. population is strongly motivated for action and achievement. The doers of this world have the "achievement motive." Although most individuals feel they have an achievement motive, there are few doers.

McClelland states that the most convincing sign of a strong achievement motive is the tendency for a person, who isn't being required to think about anything in particular, to think about ways in which to accomplish something difficult and significant. People with a strong achievement motive will think about accomplishment when free to relax with nothing else on their minds.

Learning is finding out what you already know. Doing is demonstrating that you know it.
—Richard Bach

The difference between high achievers and low achievers is high achievers think actively and not passively. Studies on high achievers indicate they can take a lot of time to just think about things. Their sense of accomplishment isn't based only on being active physically, but also on their ability to meditate, ponder, and daydream.

Achievers think about being doers and attaining a sense of accomplishment. Eventually they do what they have been planning to do; this makes the difference in their lives. They know making a difference—whether in leisure pursuits or in business affairs—means having to light the fire rather than just waiting around to be warmed by someone else's fire.

Rocks Are Hard, Water Is Wet, and Low Motivation Gets You No Satisfaction

Even though only a minority of us will motivate ourselves sufficiently to attain satisfaction in our lives, some psychologists say all of us are motivated at all times. There seems to be a contradiction here. I can think of many individuals who can't even say the word "motivation", let alone experience it.

What these psychologists are saying is that everything we do is a result of some motive. Nevertheless, many people are motivated to do little or nothing at all. I label this type of motivation as negative motivation because it influences us in directions opposite to those that we must follow to win at the game of life.

Because they are victims of their own insecurities and past failures, people with negative attitudes and low motivation in life just go through the motions. They complain all the time. They start things and don't finish them. They make the same mistakes over and over again, and nothing around them seems to work. The saddest thing is they aren't aware of how negative they really are.

The desire for comfort and the tendency to avoid taking risks usually result in low motivation or complete inaction. Although fear can be a positive motivator, it more often than not negatively motivates us to react in ways that contribute little or nothing to our satisfaction. Fear, for the most part, induces us to react negatively, rather than positively.

> I learn from my mistakes. I can make the same mistake with greater ease the second time around.
> —Unknown Wise Person

Other unhealthy modes of thinking, such as the one-big-deal syndrome, act as negative motivation. The one-big-deal syndrome is one of those adolescent-rescue fantasies we all had in our younger years. Unfortunately, I know many people who have carried these adolescent-rescue fantasies well into their fifties and sixties. Adolescent fantasies are favorites of unmotivated adults with low self-esteem.

Here are some variations of the one-big-deal syndrome: If I could only win a 5-million-dollar lottery, then I would be happy; if I could only get a new relationship with someone exciting, then I wouldn't be so bored; and if I could get an exciting, high-paying job, then I could start living. People afflicted with the one-big-deal syndrome are looking for an easy way to happiness, where none exists. Waiting for the one big deal is a means of avoiding the effort required to make life work.

> Argue for your limitations, and sure enough, they are yours.
> —Richard Bach

There are many other thinking patterns that can signal inadequate motivation in life. If you have any of the following beliefs or thoughts, you are subjecting yourself to negative motivators that will contribute absolutely nothing to your success and satisfaction.

- ➤ I have problems in life that are unique. Nobody else could possibly have these whoppers.
- ➤ You can't tell me anything that I don't already know.
- ➤ I must be liked by as many people as possible or I will be miserable. When someone dislikes me, I feel bad about myself.
- ➤ I have a right to what I want in life and shouldn't be subjected to the discomfort of failure.
- ➤ The world ought to be fair, especially to me.
- ➤ All people are so different from the way they should be.
- ➤ Changing myself is impossible because I was born this way.

- My childhood will always affect me because my less-than-perfect parents are to blame for the way I am.
- Governments don't do enough for common people like myself.
- I am disadvantaged because I don't have enough money, am not beautiful, and don't know the right people.
- I am a good person who is nice to everybody. Why isn't everyone the same way to me?

If you regularly have any of the above thoughts, you are setting yourself up for much grief and pain. You are consciously or subconsciously generating excuses for not taking the steps you must take to make your life work.

Blaming the world for being a lousy place is a good way to guarantee that the world will continue to remain lousy for you. Even when you see the light at the end of the tunnel, it will be an oncoming train. You will end up giving credence to an old Norwegian adage: "Nothing is so bad it can't get worse."

The following exercise may help put things in proper perspective about who is responsible for your satisfaction.

Exercise 7-1. The Creator of Satisfaction

Spend a few moments answering the following questions:

1. Are you willing for your life to be successful?

2. Do you want satisfaction in your life?

3. Regarding your relationship with yourself, who is the source of the experience of your satisfaction?

4. Whom do you blame if you are not attaining enjoyment and satisfaction in your life?

5. To whom do you give credit when you are successful and experience satisfaction from your accomplishments?

6. In your life, if satisfaction is missing, who is not creating this satisfaction?

The purpose of the above exercise is to remind you that you are ultimately responsible for satisfaction in your life. If you tend to blame other people or circumstances for your present state of mind, you are putting yourself at the mercy of those other people and those circumstances. You must believe that you have control over the quality of your life; if you don't, people and circumstances will conspire against your success. You can't take the attitude that, if life was a little easier, you would try to accomplish more. Life is the way it is and not the way it ought to be. Rocks are hard, water is wet, and low motivation gets you no satisfaction. You must commit yourself to action if you want things to change.

> My life is filled with many obstacles. The greatest obstacle is me.
>
> —Jack Parr

All of us, at some time or other, harbor the deep-seated hope that we will be spared the necessity of taking charge of our lives. We hope that someone else will do it for us. Life is not that way; nothing happens by itself.

Everything of major importance that you want to accomplish must be handled by yourself. To be positively motivated towards achieving greater heights, you must find a way to eliminate all your unhealthy thought processes. Healthy thought processes constitute positive motivation. When you find positive reasons for taking action, you will be well on your way to accomplishment and satisfaction.

> What is is, and what ought to be is a damn lie.
>
> —Lenny Bruce

Motivating Yourself to Climb Maslow's Ladder

Several motivational theories have been developed over the years. Probably the most famous one is that of Abraham Maslow. His theory on the hierarchy of human needs helps explain what motivates us to undertake the projects we pursue in life.

The theory of the hierarchy of needs is based on three assumptions:

1. There is a definite rank, order, priority, or hierarchy of needs that dictates our behavior.
2. The central assumption is that our higher needs may not be activated until lower needs have been reasonably satisfied.
3. We are motivated by unsatisfied needs.

There are five basic needs for which human beings strive. The needs in ascending order are:

- ➤ **Physiological needs** relate to the normal functioning of the body and include needs for water, food, rest, sex, and air.
- ➤ **Security needs** relate to our need to keep ourselves free from harm and include protection against danger, deprivation, threat, and insecurity.
- ➤ **Social needs** include our desire for love, companionship, and friendship. Overall these needs reflect our desire to be accepted by others.
- ➤ **Esteem needs** form our desire for respect and generally are divided into two categories: self-esteem and esteem from others.
- ➤ **Self-actualization needs** reflect our desire to be creative and maximize our full potential.

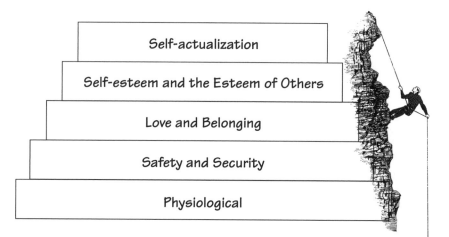

Regardless of who we are, our needs aren't static. Needs constantly change. Maslow contended that as our present needs are satisfied, other needs arise, and then these new needs dominate us. He stated that throughout our lives we are practically always desiring something. No doubt this delights most advertisers.

We are best poised to enjoy leisure when we are self-actualized. Even when we reach the state of self-actualization, we can never consider ourselves fully self-actualized. A perfect state of satisfaction would bore us to death. And, of course, it would be a nightmare for advertisers. We never reach a state of complete satisfaction for long. As one desire is eliminated, another one is waiting to replace it.

Only the shallow know themselves.
—*Oscar Wilde*

Our ability to satisfy our needs is dependent on first knowing what it is that we need; we should know our needs well. This is easier said than done. According to Maslow, we may or may not be aware of our own basic needs. He surmised, "In the average person they are more often unconscious than conscious…, although they may, with suitable techniques, and with sophisticated people, become conscious."

All of us signal our needs to the world. Often this is done subconsciously. Our needs may remain a mystery to ourselves, but not to others.

Exercise 7-2. Do You Need This Test?

Committing yourself to becoming fully aware of your behavior, attitudes, beliefs, and viewpoints will go a long way towards understanding your needs and motivations. Here is a test to determine where you are on Maslow's ladder. Although you will find Maslow mentioned in many academic books, you won't find this test mentioned in them. That's because the test was developed by a nonacademic. The test is not highly scientific, so don't take the results as being gospel.

Listed are some typical signals of each of Maslow's levels. These may help you develop a profile of the type of person you are. It will also show how far you must go to reach the ideal state for enjoying leisure, that of self-actualization.

First, analyze how you perceive yourself. Then, try to see yourself as others see you. Since we have a tendency to perceive ourselves differently from how our friends perceive us, have a friend or two evaluate you as well.

1. **Physiological Needs**
   - Not very energetic—often suffers from fatigue
   - Little or no ambition
   - Is sloppy with dress and grooming and may drive a beat-up old car
   - Prone to illness—hypochondriac
   - Loner who avoids groups
   - Self-image is very low and feels victimized by society
   - Unproductive at work

2. **Security Needs**
   - Chronic worrier who avoids taking risks
   - Negative, uncreative person who lacks confidence
   - Suffers from world-owes-me-a-living syndrome
   - Always feels his/her income is inadequate
   - Talks a lot about money, retirement plans, and insurance
   - Drives older car—its value doubles when filled with gas

> Wears clothing that went out of style years ago
> Supporter of unions who is not very productive

3. Belonging Needs

> Agreeable person—wants to be liked by everyone
> Wears up-to-date but basic clothing
> Belongs to many clubs and organizations
> Attends far too many functions and parties
> Conformist who always tries to fit in
> Takes part in many team activities
> Decent worker but not very creative

4. Ego or Esteem Needs

> Hooked on the external life
> Brags about awards and trophies
> Highly competitive at sports
> Outspoken and always seeking attention from others
> Is often a big name-dropper
> Drives an expensive car (financed to the hilt) with vanity plates

Tell me something! Is this self-actualization?

> Carries a cellular telephone into restaurants to show off
> A competitor who tries to outdo or one-up everyone
> Wears flashy brand-name clothing with lots of writing or advertising
> Is a doer who likes challenging activities and can be creative

5. Achievement or Actualization Needs

> Is self-confident and feels secure about position in society
> Creates own purpose in life
> Creative and independent—has rich internal life
> Definitely does not have vanity license plates on car
> Accepts other individuals' points of view
> Good dresser in a conservative manner
> Sociable but also likes privacy
> Not addicted to material goods for self-esteem
> Looks for quality friendships rather than quantity

Remember that the above exercise is not a scientific test. I introduced this exercise in this book to get you thinking about yourself. I don't want you losing what self-esteem you have just because you or your friend evaluated you on the lowest or second lowest rung of Maslow's ladder.

Then again, there may be something significant to consider after taking the test. You should always be looking for areas where you can improve yourself. If you didn't have what it takes to make it to the bottom rung of the ladder, you should show some concern. Even if you didn't make it to the bottom rung, there is still hope for you. You would be surprised at how many of the rest of us, at some point in our lives, had self-esteem so low that we had to stand on our tiptoes just to reach the lowest rung.

My inferiority complexes aren't as good as yours.
—Unknown Wise Person

Many people with great natural ability have been immobilized because of their inability to get their esteem out of the deep ditch in which it rested. If you have low self-esteem, it is imperative that you do what is necessary to get out of the rut and raise your concept of yourself. With low self-esteem you will continue to experience frustration and failure. Low self-esteem is a paralyzing disease that invariably produces unhappiness.

The real secret of success is enthusiasm.
—Walter Chrysler

The way to higher self-esteem is to change your attitude about the way things are and the way you are. If you can start achieving something in your life, your esteem is bound to go up. Achievements in leisure can be large or small; both will raise your esteem. With higher self-esteem you will be more motivated to go out and get what you want in life.

Do You Want What You Think You Want?

Only with effort and action can you start getting what you want in life. Keep in mind that filling your time with just any activity, when it may not have much meaning to you, isn't the route to satisfying leisure. Your opportunity for enhancing your life is dependent upon your ability to determine what your needs are and how you can best satisfy them. The following exercise requires that you answer a simple question.

Exercise 7-3. Another Simple Question

What do you really want in life?

In Richard Bach's book *Illusions,* he writes, "The simplest questions are most profound." The above question is a simple one with profound implications; it isn't an easy question to answer.

Let's say, without realizing it deep down, you really want to stay at home for your summer vacation. For a change, all you want is some rest, a lot of local sunshine, the time to read some good books, the coziness of your own home, and a daily visit to your bistro for a great cup of capuccino with your spouse.

There are a few problems: Your parents want you to go to Florida where they went for vacation. To convince you to go would validate that it was a good place for them to have gone in the first place, even though they didn't enjoy it all that much. Your friends Bob and Alice want you to go to the Rocky Mountains because that is where they are going. It would be nice for them to have someone with whom to have dinner, because they don't know what to say to each other when they are together at dinner (they have been married for over a year). Of course, your travel agent wants you to choose an exotic place such as Aruba, Martinique, Bermuda, Puerto Vallarta, or

After ten years of traveling to exotic, far-away places I realized I just wanted to vacation in my backyard.

Morocco. Your agent says she wants you to have the best possible vacation; the truth is she wants to make the biggest possible commission, so she can have the best possible vacation.

You choose to go to Martinique for two weeks because the travel agent convinces you that you deserve the best possible vacation. Everybody who is a somebody is going to Martinique, and you should show people you are a successful somebody.

Two days into the vacation, it occurs to you that you have seen all there is to see. You and your spouse lie on the beach all day being bored by watching all the other people being bored watching you. You only took one good book with you, which you have already read, and there are no good books to be purchased here. It is impossible to get a capuccino at the hotel where you are staying. The flight there and back is tiring. When you finally get home, you realize that you didn't get what you wanted from the vacation. At the end of it all, you are more tired than when you left, and you feel unfulfilled because you didn't get the vacation you wanted.

One of life's most difficult processes is discovering what we really want as individuals. Keep in mind that most of us don't know what we really want because we haven't taken the time to find out. Instead, we define our personal wants and successes according to the expectations of others. Societal standards have become more important than our own unique needs.

We pay too much attention to what others want us to want. Society wants us to want. Advertisers want us to want. Our family wants us to want. Friends want us to want. Many others, such as newspaper reporters, radio announcers, and self-serving travel agents, want us to want. Everyone wants us to want so much that most of us haven't stopped to figure out what we really want for ourselves.

> Life is a progress from want to want, not from enjoyment to enjoyment.
> —Samuel Johnson

To further complicate matters, wants have a habit of shifting with the winds. Desires are shaped by hidden needs and reshaped by mysterious forces. Too often, when we get what we want, we don't want it anymore.

If there is anything that will keep you from getting what you want, it is not knowing exactly what you want. Reaching the best destination is highly unlikely if you don't know what the destination is. You must do some soul searching and really understand yourself before you can determine what your wants and needs are. Only then can you proceed on your journey of fulfilling leisure.

Challenging Your Wants

Many of us have lost touch with what life is all about. We have sacrificed the child in us, which knew what turned us on for our own satisfaction and pleasure. If we have given up our personal desires and wishes, life has dulled us so much that we are not stimulated by anything.

You may have spent so long sacrificing the things you have always wanted to do that you no longer remember what they are. If you don't know what your true needs are, you must spend more time and effort in self-discovery. Establishing your specific needs is something you can do on your own or with help from others.

Ensure that you aren't chasing after what your mother or your best friend or Madison Avenue wants you to want. To discover what you really want, you must first write down what you think you want. Recording your wants is a way to make them more visible, so you can challenge them.

Record your perceived wants by writing them down on paper or on a blackboard, or by entering them on a computer. You have to dwell on what you think you want and find the origin of that want. Finding out whether you are the source of your wants, or whether it is something you were told you wanted, is important.

As you become aware of which wants are your own and which you were conditioned to accept, you will be better prepared to pursue your genuine interests. Perhaps you will find all of your wants were there because you were told you should have them or because you thought you should want them, but you really didn't want them. Then you have to look harder to discover your true wants. Don't shy away from this task, or you may waste the rest of your life doing what someone else wants you to do; this will not contribute to a fulfilling and happy life.

> You are never given a wish without also being given the power to make it true. You may have to work for it however.
> —Richard Bach

To repeat, write down all your wants, needs, and goals in terms of what you want to do and what you want to be. As you discover what you want, you can select those activities that truly turn you on.

Growing a Leisure Tree

The world of leisure is overflowing with opportunity. You can experience many different events, things, people, and places. The incredible variety in life offers endless possibilities for enjoyment and satisfaction.

A creative approach to selecting which leisure activities we want to pursue involves first exploring what is available and what we might want to pursue. Because our memories are not as good as we think they are, it is important to write all our ideas down before we choose those activities in which we are going to get involved.

> I'll try anything once, even Limburger cheese.
> —Thomas Edison

If you are like most people, you normally use a list to record ideas. Writing your ideas on a list may limit the number of ideas you generate. Lists are not the best tools for generating and recording ideas. There is a more powerful tool, especially useful in the initial stages of a project, for generating a number of ideas. The tool is an idea tree. It is also known as a mind map, spoke diagram, thought web, and clustering diagram. The idea tree is simple, but powerful. The surprising thing is most of us were never shown how to use an idea tree when attending our schools. I first learned about it from a waiter in a restaurant.

An idea tree is started at the center of the page by recording the goal, theme, or objective for the tree. In Figure 7-1 on the next page, "Options for My Leisure" has been written in the center of the page.

Figure 7-1. A Leisure Tree

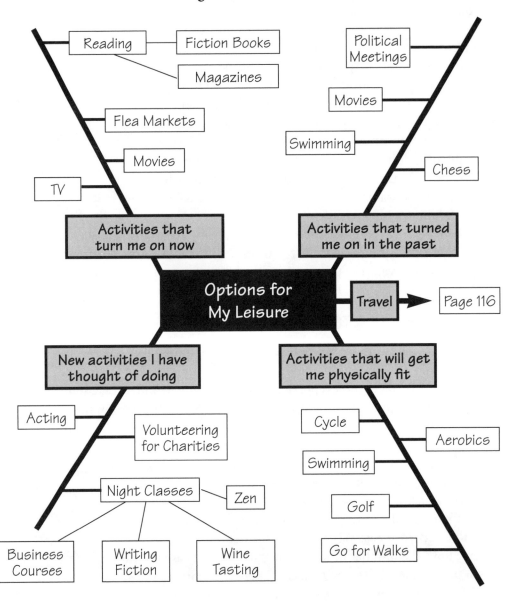

After the theme or purpose for the idea tree is recorded, branches or lines are drawn from the center towards the boundary of the page. On these branches are printed any principal ideas that relate to the objective of the tree. Principal ideas are recorded on separate branches near the center of the page.

Three important principal ideas should be used to generate ideas for leisure activities in which you may want to indulge:

1. Leisure activities that turn you on now

2. Leisure activities that have turned you on in the past

3. New leisure activities you have considered doing

Secondary branches are then drawn from the primary ones to indicate the various activities relating to the respective principal ideas. As indicated in Figure 7-1, you can add "Acting," "Volunteering for Charities," and "Night Classes" for the primary idea, "New activities I have thought of doing." More branches off the secondary ones can be drawn which will record a third level of ideas. "Zen," "Wine Tasting," "Writing Fiction," and "Business Courses" constitute the third level of ideas to enlarge on the night classes you can take. A fourth level of ideas such as "Marketing" and "Accounting" (not shown) can be added to enlarge on the business courses you may want to take.

Now is the time to start your own leisure tree, using Figure 7-1 as a guide. Utilizing the first three principal ideas, make sure you generate at least fifty things you truly like to do now, have liked to do in the past, or have thought about doing but have never got around to doing. Record every idea, no matter how frivolous it seems. Don't judge your ideas here. You have to get at least fifty, even if it takes you two days; forty-nine just won't do!

Other principal ideas can be added if you have special categories of leisure you want to actively pursue. For example, you may be very interested in getting fit and traveling in your leisure time. Then, as in Figure 7-1, you can record the principal ideas, "Activities that will get me physically fit" on one primary branch, and "Travel" on another primary branch. Note that if you run out of room, the idea tree can be expanded to another page, as this one has been for ideas on travel.

Life is a banquet, and most fools are starving to death.
—Unknown Wise Person

It is okay to have the same idea appear in more than one category. In fact, this indicates a leisure activity that may be a priority in your life. In Figure 7-1, "Swimming" appears in the categories "Activities that turned me on in the past," "Activities that will get me physically fit," and "Travel." If this was your actual leisure tree, swimming would have to be one of the first activities that you consider as a choice for pursuing immediately.

Let's look at the benefits of using the leisure tree as an idea-generating tool: First, it is compact; many ideas can be listed on one page. If needed, the idea tree can be expanded to additional pages. Second, ideas are put in categories and are easier to group. In addition, you can expand on your existing ideas to generate many new ideas.

Another advantage is the idea tree is a long-term tool. After setting it aside for a while, you can come back and generate a batch of fresh ideas. You can update it on a regular basis to ensure that you can choose from an endless number of leisure activities.

Figure 7-2. Enhanced Leisure Tree

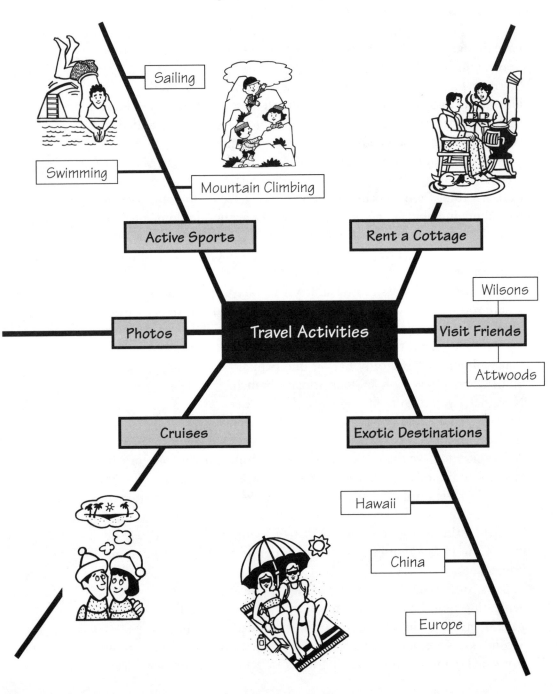

An idea tree can be enhanced by using color and images that add to our creativity and our ability to remember. Figure 7-2 shows a more advanced idea tree that uses images. As you can see, this looks a lot more interesting and useful than a conventional list.

After you have expanded your leisure tree to five or six pages, you are in a position, at any given time, to choose from a vast number of different things you can pursue in your leisure time. If you have any zest for living, you should have written enough to keep you busy for five lifetimes. If you didn't write down enough for at least two lifetimes, you have taken the easy way out. Go back and do it right! If you have trouble generating ideas for your leisure tree, refer to the list of activities on the next three pages. Your leisure tree should have enough on it so you are never at a loss for something to keep you occupied.

Exercise 7-4. Ensure You Aren't out of Your Tree

Finding the right activities for your leisure-time enjoyment is a personal matter. You may overlook many activities in which you have been involved or that you have forgotten about over time. Following is a list of over 200 leisure activities for you to consider. Go through this list and rate them using the following system:

1. Turn me on now
2. Have turned me on in the past
3. New activities I have thought of doing
4. Have no interest in the activity

Activities in categories 1, 2, and 3 interest you and belong on your leisure tree. As you add these activities to your tree, they may trigger new ideas that you will also want to put on the tree. In no time your leisure tree should have enough to keep you from getting bored for a long time. With all you have to keep you occupied, you may not get around to finishing this book.

Once you have created a leisure tree of activities, it is time to start participating in some of these activities. If you have enough for a lifetime or two, you must set priorities for those you want to pursue. It will be impossible to do them all at once. One way to prioritize your list is to think of what you would do if you had only a limited amount of time to live.

Activities For Your Leisure Tree

Play an instrument
Learn how to play an instrument
Walk
Run
Volunteer

Prepare a meal for yourself
Learn how to cook
Create a new recipe
Visit present friends
Visit old friends
Try to meet new friend
Go hiking
Write letters to celebrities
Take a survey
Sleep
Meditate
Drive around in the city
Drive in the country
Count the items in this list to see if I
    have 200
Read books
Listen to the radio
Watch television
Listen to the stereo
Travel

Go to the movies
Make a movie
Learn computing
Write a computer program
Play tennis
Paint your house
Golf
Fish
Walk through a stream barefoot
Go camping
Climb a mountain
Become involved in politics
Ride a bicycle
Ride a motorcycle

Invite friends to your home
Invent a new game
Go to the library
Search out your family tree
Play with children
Get on a talk show
Offer to work for nothing
Play billiards
Dance alone for relaxation
Dance with someone else
Take dancing lessons
Restore an old car
Restore a piece of furniture
Renovate your house
Clean your house
Telephone old friends
Write a book
Write in your diary
Create a new cartoon
Write your autobiography
Make a dress, hat, etc.
Try to create an interesting wardrobe
    for only fifty dollars
Start a collection of…
Pan for gold
Sunbathe
Swim
Have sex
Go to church
Dive in the water
Go scuba diving
Go snorkeling
Get a pilot's licence
Take up photography
Develop a photo album
Find out what a rebus is and create ten
    of your own
Find out what was happening the day
    you were born

Have a garage sale

Rearrange your living-room furniture

Take up acting

Write a play

Fly a kite

Learn to run backwards

Learn to impersonate someone famous

Plant a garden

Ride a horse

Pick some flowers

Write poetry

Write a letter to a friend

Attempt a record for running backwards

Learn how to sing

Write a song

Memorize a poem

Join an encounter group

Learn famous quotations

Memorize a song

Gaze at the stars

Truly experience a sunset

Watch the moon

Learn about new religions

Build a house

Design a unique house

Go live in another country

Go sailing

Play hockey

Build a boat

Watch interesting court cases at the courthouse

Learn more about the stock market

Invent a better mousetrap

Start a new club

Window shop

Learn how to repair your car

Throw a dinner party for a variety of people

See how many strangers will say hello to you

Shop for clothes

Watch people in public

Roller skate

Play cards

Telephone a talk show to voice your opinion

Have a candlelight dinner with someone

Join a club to improve your public speaking

Join a wine-tasting club to learn about wine

Go back to university or college to get a degree

Take up skydiving

Learn all about health and fitness

Pick fruit in an orchard

Visit local tourist sights

Take up a new hobby

Create your own palindrome

Help fight pollution

Go to a flea market

Take a catnap

Go to garage sales

Climb a tree

Go to horse races with ten dollars

Ride public transit for fun

Start a newsletter

Write a letter to a pen pal in another country

Walk in the wilderness

Do crossword puzzles

Start and operate a bed and breakfast

Build a swimming pool

Daydream

Attend a sports event

Travel to old haunts

Go white-water rafting

Go on a hot-air balloon ride

Be a big sister/brother

Go to your favorite restaurant

Try a new restaurant

Have a massage

Go to a tennis ranch to improve your tennis

Teach your dog new tricks

Learn a new trick to show your dog

Attend live theater

See the symphony

Go to a retreat to relax

Truly communicate with someone special today

Enter your favorite recipe in a contest

Invent a new product

Play with your pet

Train your mind to be creative

Run for political office

Visit a zoo

Make your own wine

Kick the television habit

Raise your vocabulary

Learn how to read financial statements

Learn how to judge personalities better

Improve your personality

End the evening by reflecting on your day

Start a new charity

Study clouds

Make a list of all the successes in your life

Play a prank on a friend

Dream up new pranks

Take twice as much time as usual to eat

Go bird-watching

Create a new game

Try doing nothing

Visit a museum

Join a new club

Go play bingo

Fly a kite

Skip rope

Start an argument

Watch someone work

Lie on a beach

Wash and polish your car

Start a hobby farm

Check this list to see if an activity is repeated

Help fight crime

Learn about solar energy

Write a book on leisure

Learn how to hypnotize yourself

Have your palm read

Do a jigsaw puzzle

Visit a craft show

Learn a magic act

Cook a lousy meal for someone not to enjoy

Learn to speak French, Spanish, etc.

Care for someone ill

Be a philosopher

Be nasty to politicians

Expand this list to 500 activities to outdo me

Exercise 7-5. Six Months to Enjoy Yourself

Assume you have been told you have six months to live. From your list of activities on your idea tree, select those items you would consider as essential to do in those six months.

The activities you chose in the above exercise should mean the most to you. You should immediately start pursuing those you have listed; tomorrow or next week is not good enough. We must remember that life does not go on forever. None of us ever knows if we only have six months or less to live. By concentrating on the list of your favorite goals and activities, you will get to do what most turns you on and gives you the most satisfaction.

Goaling for It

If you were to walk in a clockwise direction on the walls of the object depicted in the figure to the right, you would think you were going up.

It would appear to you that you were destined for greater heights. However, in no time, you would realize that you are back at the same level at which you started. No matter how much energy you put into walking up the steps, higher levels would just be illusions. Your unfocused activity would leave you without any accomplishment and satisfaction.

Such is the illusion of activity without goals and dreams. Many people misconstrue their unplanned activity for a direction in life. Even if they put substantial energy into these non-goals, they still end up getting nowhere. Activity is necessary for reaching greater heights, but greater heights only come with defined goals. If we are to arrive at new and worthwhile destinations, first we must define these destinations. The journey has direction once the destination is set.

Defined goals give us something to pursue that we otherwise wouldn't pursue—they give us purpose. When we have purpose and direction, we have reasons for being innovative and creative. Goal setting takes effort and discipline. Once goals have been established, more effort and discipline are required in working towards the goals. Then even more effort and discipline are required to monitor the goals and set new ones. Due to all the effort and discipline required, many people decide against setting goals and working towards them. Goals need an action plan to get us going. This tells us what we are going to do to get to where we are going. The action plan defines the activities in which we have to indulge while we pursue our goals.

If you have defined your leisure goals, sooner or later your wants and desires will change. Some goals will have been reached and some activities will no longer turn you on. This will necessitate a revision in your list of favorite goals and activities. It is a good idea to do a review every few weeks.

Your challenge, and not anyone else's, is to find, accept, and develop who you can be as an individual. You must face reality and accept that absolutely everything worth attaining in life—adventure, a relaxed mind, love, spiritual fulfillment, satisfaction, and happiness—has a price. Anything that enhances your existence will take action and effort. If you think otherwise, you certainly will be in for much frustration.

One of the strongest characteristics of genius is the power of lighting its own fire.
—John Foster

Remember that it is more satisfying to climb mountains than to slide down them sitting on your butt. Sitting around waiting for someone else to light the fire doesn't work. Lighting your own fire—instead of waiting around to be warmed by someone else's—will make this lifetime (and other lifetimes beyond this one if you believe in reincarnation) worth living.

CHAPTER 8

Dynamic Inaction Will Get You Nowhere

You May Be Living, but Are You Alive?

A dull-looking man walked into the bar and said to the bartender, "Make me a zombie!" The bartender took one look at him and replied, "I can't. God beat me to it!"

Many people are like this bartender's customer. They spend all their leisure time in passive activities rather than having a good balance between passive and active activities. Due to their inactivity, they are not really alive. Neither are they dead; they are somewhere in between, zombies at best.

Dynamic inaction isn't the monopoly of a few bureaucrats. Many people practice dynamic inaction in their leisure time, and it gets them nowhere. There is no limit to what these people will do so they can indulge in doing nothing or close to nothing. The problem is that after forty or fifty years of boredom they are still in the same tunnel, without any cheese, wondering when the plots in their life stories will thicken.

> *Action may not always bring happiness; but there is no happiness without action.*
> —*Benjamin Disraeli*

Because people have leisure time, it doesn't mean they know how to use it properly; just like owning a car doesn't mean one knows how to drive it properly. Over the years, the pleasures of urban populations have become largely passive: watching videos at home, watching football and hockey games, and listening to the radio. There was a reason for people to pursue passive leisure in the past: Active energies during the industrial revolution were fully expended in manual work. However, this isn't a valid reason for most working people today; a vast majority of people don't work at physical tasks. Furthermore, the ones who still do manual work don't have to work as hard because of the machines they have at their disposal.

The main reason most people are passive in their leisure is laziness. Most people look for the easiest way to spend spare time. Even in the 1930s, when people had more physical work, leisure was more active than it is today. People spent their time reading, going outside the home to movies, and dancing. North Americans have become a nation of spectators rather than a nation of doers. Individuals spend ten times more time watching television than pursuing active leisure. When people make it out of the home, they aren't necessarily more active. Studies indicate that, after the home and the workplace, shopping malls are the number one place where people spend their spare time. Researchers have determined that about 90 percent of North Americans today are reactive and passive. Instead of indulging in activities that are active in nature, they choose the most passive.

> *Leisure may prove to be a curse rather than a blessing, unless education teaches a flippant world leisure is not a synonym for entertainment.*
> —*William J. Bogan*

What's wrong with passive activities? Quality leisure is dependent upon accomplishment and self-fulfillment, which come from activities that are challenging or have some purpose. Passive activities seldom, if ever, give us the mental highs that do away with boredom. These activities are typified by no challenge, no purpose, low arousal, monotony, and lack of novelty. Although these predictable and safe activities provide security and safety, we get little or no satisfaction and self-fulfillment from them. If our passive activities aren't complemented by active ones, we won't experience quality leisure. Here are some examples of passive activities:

- ➤ Watching television
- ➤ Getting drunk or stoned
- ➤ Junking out on food

- Going for a drive
- Shopping
- Spending money
- Gambling
- Spectator sports

I want to stress that not all passive activities should be eliminated altogether. There is a time and place for many passive activities. For example, there can be a lot of good in just spontaneously goofing off with no particular purpose in mind. Passive activities are okay when done in moderation and when they complement a contingent of active activities.

He did nothing in particular, and did it very well.
—W.S. Gilbert

Activity is essential to happiness and longevity. People must realize that activities that mentally and physically involve the participants, such as going bowling or writing a novel, are much more exciting and satisfying than passive activities such as watching TV. Even leisure pursuits like daydreaming, meditation, reflection, and fantasizing are active in nature—much more so than watching television. Studies have shown that adults who remain active in leisure are more likely to exhibit higher states of physical and psychological well-being. Some activities more active in nature are:

- Writing
- Reading
- Exercising
- Walking in the park
- Painting a picture
- Playing music
- Dancing
- Taking a course

Leisure should be something we all cherish and cultivate. It affords us the opportunity to experience pleasure, enjoyment, relaxation, fulfillment, and achievement. Satisfaction in life is attained when we are able to challenge and extend our talents and abilities. Activities requiring

I always wanted to be an artist in my spare time. Now if I could only remember if I'm supposed to use my right brain or left brain.

at least moderate risk and energy will give us more satisfaction than those requiring little or no risk and energy.

A Case of Mind over Matter

Social conditioning can be a detriment to the leisure choices people make. A sure way to get old and inactive is to accept and adopt the thinking prevalent in society about what getting old signifies. Most people don't question what is said in the media, television, and books. Consequently, they believe getting older translates into having to give up most active activities. These people end up being affected by ageism, the existence of age-related myths. These myths support a passive lifestyle after people turn fifty or sixty, when a more active and satisfying life is still possible. Responses from participants in retirement planning programs indicate that most people expect to increase their passive activities once they retire. Few intend to start new activities that are active in nature.

The ability to choose an active lifestyle is mostly a case of mind over matter. Provided the person is not physically immobilized, age shouldn't be used as an excuse to give up activity. Here again, attitude jumps back into the picture. The person's attitude is important in determining whether the person pursues leisure with substantial activity. Ken Dychtwald, in his book *Age Wave*, looked at the challenges and opportunities facing an aging America. In the book, he relates the responses from the participants in his aging seminars to a question concerning what is the single most important ingredient in whether someone aged well. The participants invariably agreed that the most essential determinant of successful aging is attitude.

What is mind? No matter.
What is matter? Never mind.

—T.H. Key

Dychtwald cites many people in their sixties, seventies, and eighties who are running marathons, playing tennis, swimming, and cycling for up to eight hours a day on a regular basis, sometimes every day. Unfortunately, these active individuals are still in the minority; most North Americans let themselves go with age. This is a conditioned response more than a necessary one. In the final analysis, this can be attributed to laziness. The average U.S. senior walks about 25 miles a year. Even the average Canadian senior, who walks about 75 miles a year, is lazy compared to the average Danish senior, who walks 265 miles a year.

Watching Television Can Get You Killed

North America's most time-consuming pastime is watching television. Surveys indicate that North Americans utilize an incredible 40 percent of their leisure time watching television. No wonder people have insufficient time for exercising, visiting friends, and watching sunsets. The North American adult between eighteen and sixty-five has forty hours of spare time a week and spends sixteen hours of it in front of the tube. In comparison, only two hours are spent reading and four hours are spent talking to relatives, friends, and acquaintances.

If a man watches three football games in a row, he should be declared legally dead.
—*Erma Bombeck*

Ironically, on a list of twenty-two leisure activities, TV viewing rated seventeenth on the amount of enjoyment and satisfaction attained. Reading was rated ninth on this list. Why do people watch television if they get so little satisfaction from the activity? People choose television viewing because it is the easy thing to do. Of course, because of television's low rate of return in terms of satisfaction, the easy route turns out to be difficult and uncomfortable in the long term.

Like workaholism, excessive television watching is a harmful addiction. It has been billed *The Plug-In Drug* by writer Marie Winn. Although television can be educational and informative, there are many negative aspects associated with watching too much: it can even get you killed by your immediate family. The UPI news service in December 1990 reported that a Florida man's family confessed to trying unsucussfully to kill him several times before succeeding. They eventually shot him dead because he was a miserable, grouchy man who spent all his spare time lying on the couch watching television. The man's daughter stated, "He'd come home from work and all he'd do is lay on the couch and watch TV. That's all he did. Like, he never did anything."

I find television very educating. Every time somebody turns on the set I go into the other room and read a book.
—*Groucho Marx*

Exercise 8-1. How to Make TV Fulfilling

Although watching television is a highly passive activity, there is one sure way to spend endless hours each month in front of a television set and still have fulfilling and rewarding leisure time in great measure. What is the one way? (See the end of this chapter—page 140—for the answer.)

Besides TV-watching's inherent passivity, it is harmful for other reasons. Many programs and commercials depict life in a way that isn't real. This contributes to distorted pictures of the world and fantasies about life that can't be realized.

If you watch television excessively, cutting down on your viewing hours is an opportunity to enhance your leisure time. I can't tell you how much television is the right amount for you; it's your leisure time and your life. If you watch television to a large degree, and your life isn't what you think it should be, then doing something more challenging and fulfilling is probably the answer.

TV-free America is a newly established national organization based in Washington that raises awareness of the harmful effects of excessive television watching. The organization recommends that, instead of watching television, people should spend their time in more productive activities, such as contemplating life, playing sports, attending community events, and volunteering. If you are addicted to television, it is time to join a support group such as Couch Potatoes (see resources). Getting away from the television set and into activities promoted by the Institute of Totally Useless Skills—feather balancing, paper-airplane making, napkin stunts, pen bouncing, creative beer-can crushing, or generating symptoms of false physical self-abuse—will do you more good than watching most television programs.

Don't Weight Too Long to Control Your Wait

Harold, you can't solve all your problems by watching reruns of All in the Family, *and adopting the philosophy of Archie Bunker.*

No person is an island, but some people come pretty close with their constant nibbling on chips, nachos, peanuts, grass, trees, and anything else they get their hands on. Junking out on food is a passive activity in which many people get very active. Overeating goes hand in hand with television watching. Both activities, especially when combined and done to an excess, can lead people to an early death.

Life is too good in North America; far too many people are overweight. In the early 1960s less than a quarter of the U.S. population was obese. The President's Council of Physical Fitness and Sports concluded that in the early 1990s over a third of the population was obese. Even people we expect to be fit aren't. A 1996 study by the Ontario Heart and Stroke Foundation found that despite the image of baby boomers as an exercise-crazed generation, they are in some ways less healthy than their parents were at the same age.

Being overweight will interfere with your ability to enjoy many great pleasures in life. A good way to become overweight is to come up with excuses for putting on those extra pounds. Here is a good one if you don't already have enough excuses to justify your overeating: I recently heard a deejay on a local radio station report that a doctor claimed it was normal for people to gain three pounds a year after they were thirty. This is another case in which people, both the doctor who made this statement and the deejay who repeated it, have not overworked their brain cells thinking too much. This statement not only is ridiculous, but dangerous. If I allowed myself to put on three pounds a year, by the time I was sixty-five I would weigh 275 pounds and have a perfect look-alike body to Dom DeLuise's in the movie *Fatso*. The doctor's statement also suggests people in their eighties, who weigh a comfortable 170 pounds, must have weighed only fifty pounds when they were forty.

> I went on a diet, swore off drinking and heavy eating, and in fourteen days I lost two weeks.
> —Joe E. Lewis

The Washington Post, in January 1996, reported that even though most people put on weight as they grow older, the latest U.S. government guidelines (issued jointly by the Department of Agriculture and the Human Service Department) say waistlines should not automatically increase with age. The new guidelines include one weight chart for men and women and no longer make age-related distinctions for adults. One official was reported to state that people should not gain more than ten pounds after they have reached adult height, which normally occurs at about age twenty-one.

> I am not going to starve to death just so I can live a little longer.
> —Irene Peter

There are many excuses available for gaining weight. With excuses the battle against the bulge is easily lost. Although gaining a pound or two with age may be unavoidable, you can control your weight through exercise and diet. I have designated the weight I am comfortable with and have worked hard to maintain it at this level for many years. Your duty is to do the same if you want to feel good about yourself. The best way to accomplish this is by being as active as possible in the more active leisure activities.

Are You Exercising All Your Excuses for Not Exercising?

If you enjoy good health, you are in a position to undertake many more active activities than if you have poor health. Good health is a richness you should not take for granted. The way to maintain your good health (and your right weight) is through regular exercise. A study done by researchers from the Institute for Aerobics Research in Dallas, as reported in the *Journal of the American Medical Association,* showed strong evidence that physically fit people live longer. Even moderate exercise can improve your health substantially. Compared to the most fit men, the least fit men had more than triple the death risk. For women, the least fit had quadruple the death risk as the most fit.

Give a man a fish and he eats for a day. Teach him how to fish and you get rid of him for the whole weekend.

—*Zenna Schaffer*

The University of California *Wellness Letter* stated in 1992 that 18 percent of people in Montana and 52 percent of people in the District of Columbia had reported no participation in any leisure-time physical activity during the previous month. I become disgusted with myself if I have no leisure-time physical activity for two days, let alone a month. A few years ago, I thought I could get away with eating like a horse and not exercising. Darn it! No such luck. I found out, when the post office was about to give me my own postal code because of my size, that eating excessively while not exercising was going to cost me a new wardrobe, not to mention the not-so-insignificant items of health and wellness. For the last fifteen years, I have exercised twice a day, for a total of at least two hours, by participating in vigorous activities such as tennis, jogging, and cycling. Of course, some lazy, unfit people now tell me how lucky I am because I don't have a weight problem.

Those who do not find time for exercise will have to find time for illness.

—*Unknown Wise Person*

All of us have the opportunity to get fit through regular exercise, yet only a small minority of us is fit. Despite evidence that physical activity is a key to robust health, long life, and physical attraction, the 1996 U.S. Surgeon General's *Report on Physical Activity and Health* concludes that at least 60 percent of adults aren't active enough. *USA TODAY* in July 1996 reported that "we are a nation of sloths." Only 22 percent of Americans meet the minimum requirement of thirty minutes of moderate activity most days of the week.

You aren't going to get fit by casually riding a bicycle at two miles per hour or going for a fifteen-minute walk while window shopping. A 1995 Harvard University study shows that only vigorous activity sustained for longer periods will get you fit. The study, which linked vigorous exercise to longevity, indicated that playing a standard round of golf couldn't be considered a vigorous workout. Similarly, gardening for a half hour is better than nothing; however, this won't get you fit. The benefit is just that—a little better than nothing!

The American College of Sports Medicine recommends twenty to sixty minutes of continuous aerobic activity three or more times a week for optimal fitness. An example of what will get you in shape, and add to your longevity, is walking at four to five miles an hour for forty-five minutes at a time. You must do this several times a week. Fitness will be achieved only if you are involved in activities that get your cardiovascular system going. A half-hour of intense walking, jogging, swimming, dancing, hiking, or cycling should be the minimum. You will know you are getting some benefit if your workout gets you perspiring for at least twenty minutes.

It is no wonder that most people aren't fit. According to the National Sporting Goods Association, there are 90 million Americans who exercise fewer than two days a month. They all have their excuses; the top five excuses in order are:

1. Not enough time
2. Not enough discipline
3. Can't find an interesting activity
4. Can't find a partner
5. Can't afford the equipment

When it comes to excuses, pay heed to something Mark Twain said: "One thousand excuses and no good reasons." If you are using the above excuses, remember these are not reasons. Excuses are for people who don't want to take responsibility. Let's look at the nature of these excuses.

The issue of "not enough time" is normally a case of poor time management. This can be handled by creating the time. Acknowledging how many hours a day you are wasting watching television creates an opportunity to substitute exercise during those times. Of course, then you

If I had known I was going to live this long,
I would have taken better care of myself.

have to be disciplined to go out and exercise. The second excuse, "not enough discipline," definitely signifies laziness. You have to take action because no one can do it for you. It takes effort and practice to overcome laziness or lack of discipline.

"Can't find an interesting activity" is as shallow an excuse as can be found. First, use your creativity. There are a thousand and one different ways to exercise. If you can't find one interesting physical activity, it is not that all activities are boring; it is you who are boring. The excuse, "can't find a partner," is also very shallow. This can be overcome easily by doing those exercises you can do alone. There are many such activities. If you can't do things alone because you fear loneliness, Chapter 10 provides some food for thought on this topic.

Using the excuse "can't afford the equipment" demonstrates limited thinking. Contrary to what advertisers want you to believe, exercising does not require expensive equipment. There are many things you can do that will cost practically nothing. If you live in a relatively cold climate, as I do, be creative and think about various things you can do indoors during the cold days. The latest fashions in clothing aren't essential, unless you believe you may wind up as a contestant in a fashion contest while jogging or playing ball in the park. Advertisers want you to believe the latest fashions are important to make a statement about who you are. If you think you need the latest fashions to make a statement about who you are while exercising, new equipment or new fashions are definitely not what you need. What you need is a course in self-esteem.

Other excuses that people use for not exercising are:

➤ I am too old to begin
➤ It's too cold outside
➤ I am twenty years old and don't need to exercise
➤ I don't want to sustain an injury

If you use any of these excuses, you are just fooling yourself. These are excuses and not reasons. You are using the excuses to cover up your laziness. The key here is to forget about the excuses. Just go out and do it; this takes care of the excuses every time.

If you think that you are a little too old to exercise because you are now in your forties or fifties, think again! Every year on his birthday, a youthful man from Ontario runs the same number of kilometers as his age. You are probably thinking, "this is no big deal for a man in his twenties, but wait until he reaches forty. He will never be able to keep it up."

> I like long walks, especially when they are taken by people who annoy me.
> —Fred Allen

Wrong! Joe Womersley didn't start running until he was fifty-two years old, at which time he was considerably overweight, unfit, and a heavy smoker.

I first heard about Joe Womersley on CBC radio's *Morningside* program with Peter Gzowski. In September of 1994, Joe turned sixty-nine and ran sixty-nine kilometers (forty-two miles) and in September, 1995, on his seventieth birthday, he was shooting for seventy kilometers. In a scheduled twenty-six-mile marathon run on Baffin Island in 1994, Joe ran fifty-two miles because he felt twenty-six miles was for "wimps." Proving he can complete long marathons and encouraging others to get fit, no matter what their age, is Joe's passion. Joe has run over 120 marathons since he started at the age of fifty-two.

If you work at a regular job, an excuse that may pop up is that after work you are too tired to exercise. Often you need exercise the most when you don't feel like exercising. Normally, you are feeling mental fatigue; this will be alleviated by physical exercise. Half the battle is just getting out there for the first ten minutes. After that, the next forty-five minutes or hour are relatively easy. In fact, after ten or twenty minutes exercise can become so enjoyable that you actually will end up exercising longer than you had intended.

There is a reason for this: While we exercise, our bodies release hormones called endorphins into the bloodstream. The result is a natural high that puts us in a state of euphoria. This natural high helps eliminate that feeling of being down. Surprisingly, the physical activity eliminates the feeling of boredom that made us feel like not exercising in the first place.

If the television, the couch, and the fridge have become your three best friends, you must take action now. Establish a fitness program and stick to it. Exercise will keep you healthy and in a better mood to be more active in other activities. Individuals with good health are likely to pursue active leisure, while people with bad health are likely to pursue passive leisure. Exercising regularly and becoming fit will have a profound impact on your happiness and well-being. Your physical skills and abilities will be maintained far longer if you get out and exercise your body on a regular basis. It is a case of use it or lose it. You can't stop the aging process, but you can certainly slow it down with exercise. The important point about exercising is getting out there and doing it.

Smart Minds Ask Dumb Questions

We regularly condition our houses. We regularly condition our cars. We regularly condition our bicycles. Some of us even regularly condition our bodies, but few of us regularly condition our minds. Regularly conditioning our minds can be as beneficial as regularly conditioning our bodies. Many people are in good physical condition, but their minds aren't in great condition. The ability to think critically and creatively is a rarely developed ability. What passes for thinking in our society is usually no more than the regurgitation of old facts and figures that were reported in the media or by someone else.

Great minds have purposes, others have wishes.

—Washington Irving

As children, we asked many dumb questions. We were curious and saw much wonder in this world. As adults, we can continue to challenge our minds with the new and mysterious. We should ask at least one dumb question a day. There can be much wonder and many new things to ponder until the day we die. We don't know everything there is to know (although a lot of us think we do). In fact, dumb minds have an answer for everything, while smart minds regularly ask dumb questions. With so many interesting things about which we can think and ask questions, there is no reason for our minds to become rusty. If you can't generate your own mysteries to contemplate at this moment, here are five to get you started:

> ➤ What is another word for thesaurus?
> ➤ Why do we drive on a parkway and park on a driveway?
> ➤ Why are your toes in front of your feet instead of behind them?
> ➤ Why does a cow stand still while a farmer burglarizes her?
> ➤ Why is this question in itself a dumb question?

Another way to condition our minds is to take part in continuing education courses offered at our colleges and universities. Taking a course can be an extremely rewarding activity whether you are employed or unemployed. One of the most rewarding courses I have ever taken is a wine tasting course. Talk about enjoyable! It conditioned my mind in a different way than other courses have. In what other course can you get to sip wine from a glass half an hour into every class and learn something at the same time?

Here are some benefits from taking courses:

> Self-esteem is increased

> Great place to meet new friends

> Enhances personal growth and self-awareness

> Improves mental dexterity

> Helps you prepare for going back to work

> Assists in handling the rapid changes with which we have to deal

Universities are full of knowledge; the freshmen bring a little in and the seniors take none away, and knowledge accumulates.

—Lawrence Lowell

A creative mind is an active mind, and an active mind asks many questions. Only through active questioning can we keep our minds developing and discovering new ways of thinking. Questioning our values, questioning our beliefs, and questioning why we are doing things the way we are doing them should be normal. Socrates, a great thinker in his time, encouraged his students to question everything, including what he was teaching them. You should use your mind in active ways to ensure you are not letting it rust away. Here again, just like with your body, you must use it or lose it!

Be a Traveler Instead of a Tourist

Travel, when done right, will broaden and refresh your outlook on life. Experiencing new people, new customs, new surroundings, and new ways to live will enrich your life. The important consideration is to travel actively. On my trip to Saint Lucia I was stunned by the number of people on the beach who didn't look like they were having a good time. I was puzzled since most people had come such a long way in order to enjoy themselves. Except for my girlfriend and a family from Germany, no one was very excited about anything. Everyone seemed to be spending their week or two on the beach watching everyone else not having a good time.

There are three things difficult: to suffer an injury; to keep a secret; and to use leisure.

—Voltaire

If you can, avoid signing up for tour packages in which a tour guide takes you from place to place. This is passive traveling; there is much more to travel. Don't be a tourist. Instead, try being a true traveler like Jim MacKenzie, my schoolteacher friend, who takes sabbaticals every four or five years.

Tourists are passive and constitute the package-deal crowd. They opt for the one- or two-week getaways. On these package deals they are constrained by fixed schedules and the obligation to conform to the group. Jim, as a traveler, is more creative and adventurous than tourists. He chooses his own destination and isn't bound by any schedule. Not having to compromise for a group's common purpose, he can take his time to explore and enjoy the country that he is visiting. Because he can be more spontaneous, the vacation is more unpredictable and interesting.

When you want to learn about a country, be a traveler and go where most tourists don't go. Talk to the local people if you know their language. Learn how they view life. Carry a camera and take many pictures. Record all the interesting events in your diary. Incidentally, when you get off the beaten paths and go to the out-of-the-way places, you stand a good chance to find the excellent restaurants not frequented by tourists. Find out where the locals dine, and you will be in for a culinary delight.

A drive in the country isn't too exciting.

This will be. The country is Mexico.

If you want to go to some out-of-the-way destinations, search them out in the Lonely Planet guides. Tony Wheeler, an international-travel writer and publisher of the Lonely Planet travel guides, is quoted in the *Book Of Lists* as recommending these destinations along with others as worthwhile places to visit: Hanoi, Mexico City, Calcutta, Monaco, Nagasaki, and Belfast. The reputations of these places may not be great, but Wheeler recommends them because they have a lot to offer. For example, about Calcutta he says, "It is never boring and has an infectious zest for life."

Another active way to travel is to get involved in a volunteer vacation. This can be a fun-filled and rewarding experience. You don't have to go overseas for this. There are many volunteer vacation programs all over the United States. You get to offer your work to organizations that can use your skills and abilities. The benefits to you are the adventure and the satisfaction you gain from helping others less fortunate than you.

Remember that you don't have to travel far to have a vacation. Don't overlook the place where you live because it doesn't compare to somewhere else you have visited or lived. Every town or city has its unique features that many of its residents ignore or don't appreciate. Visit your own city to discover its fascinating features. Take your time in getting to know the ethnic restaurants, the sunsets, the biking trails, the architecture, the storefronts, the different neighborhoods, and the parks. You may discover paradise in your own backyard.

Try Reading, Writing, or. . .

Two more active leisure activities can add immensely to the quality in our leisure time: reading and writing. Few people indulge in either one.

Unfortunately, there has been a general decline in reading, both in quantity and quality (undoubtedly, some academics will direct partial blame at me because of the quality of my books). Although Americans and Canadians purchase many books, even most copies of bestsellers wind up being used as doorjambs rather than reading material. Tom Peters estimated that only 1 million of the 5 million people who bought his bestseller, *In Search Of Excellence*, even bothered to open the book, and only 100,000 read the book from cover to cover.

> *The man who doesn't read good books has no advantage over the man who can't read them.*
> —Mark Twain

Whether it's Duthie's in Vancouver or City Lights in San Francisco, a bookstore offers incredible treasures. Every public library is also a literary gold mine. Reading books purchased in bookstores or borrowed from libraries is one of those active and satisfying indulgences everyone should pursue. Yet I read somewhere that statistics indicate the average university graduate in the United States reads about one book a year after graduation. Only 3 percent of the American population own library cards. In the United States and Canada, only 20 percent of the population spends leisure time reading.

Why a greater proportion of the population doesn't read books is a question I have often pondered. Most people may as well be illiterate for the amount they read. Apparently people find reading books too difficult. The Easy Rule of Life from Chapter 6 applies here; doing the more difficult activities would give them more satisfaction.

> *Employ your time in improving yourself by other people's writings, so you shall come easily by what others have labored hard for.*
> —Socrates

Reading is the fastest way to gain knowledge and wisdom about the world in which we live. If you want to take the shortest route to success in any field of endeavor, then read the works of great philosophers. This is the easiest (and cheapest I might add) way to acquire the wisdom and knowledge that will make you a winner at work or play.

Writing takes a little more effort than reading. By taking time to write letters or books, you get to express your opinions and your creativity. Writing letters is something all of us could do more frequently. If you like receiving letters, then you should write. That way you will get more in return. Writing letters can be satisfying if you express your creativity. Add anything, such as quotes or drawings, that makes your letters different. The person to whom you write will be pleasantly surprised with your letter, which isn't the run-of-the-mill variety.

When one has no particular talent for anything, one takes to the pen.
—Honoré de Balzac

Writing a book is more difficult than writing a letter. However, just because something is difficult is no reason for not doing it. I encounter many people who dream of writing a book but never get around to it because of their excuses. If you want to write a book, then do it. Here again, if I can do it, so can you. I should point out I failed my first-year university English course three times before I finally passed it; I am still able to write books. Start by putting in at least fifteen minutes a day. This is how this book was started. Even if you do just this bare minimum, you still will have progressed towards completion.

I can't wait to get older, so I can be like the rest of the grown-ups, and read only one book a year.

Once you have written a book, publish it on your own if you believe in it. Many books that went on to be bestsellers were self-published. But don't equate success with making it a bestseller. If your book is enjoyed by one person other than yourself, it is a success; anything over and above this is a bonus.

I feel that only illiterate and lazy individuals don't relish reading and writing. Of course, I may be wrong. You may not be lazy or illiterate but still not enjoy reading and writing. Then try something from the myriad of other active activities you can pursue.

Action Is Eloquence

Once you understand that your attitude and energy determine the quality of your leisure, you will be on your way to creating the events and situations that help you live life to the fullest. William Shakespeare said, "Action is eloquence." As an action-oriented person, you will handle the inertia that stops the majority from pursuing active leisure. Overcoming inertia is the way to become creatively alive. Taking the steps to do something that is highly active goes a long way towards eliminating depression, anxiety, and stress.

When it comes to life, two kinds of people exist: participants and spectators. Some people spend most of their time making things happen and some people spend their time watching what happens. If you spend most of your time watching what is happening, it won't be long before your life is over and you will be wondering what happened.

Absentmindedly pursuing leisure in ways such as watching endless television is a sure way to become bored and physically and mentally unfit. Always killing time will only serve to kill you faster. If your leisure repertoire doesn't include a good balance of passive and active activities, chances are you are not going to be very happy. The best cure for boredom is finding out which activities you are passionate about. The activities that give you the most satisfaction are those which challenge you and provide you with a purpose. If an activity is really stimulating, we tend to lose track of time and place while we are involved in it.

> Be content to act, and leave the talking to others.
> —Baltasar Gracián

There must be several things you are passionate about. Maybe you are excited about mountain climbing or gardening or skydiving or riding horses or collecting old coins. The important thing is to have the enthusiasm that is so vital to getting you involved in something active. If you are passionate about what you do, you will show more vitality, more interest, and more radiance.

Exercise 8-2. Measuring Your Passion

Go back to your leisure tree or list of leisure activities that you have considered pursuing. Rate these activities on a Passion Index of one (practically no desire) to five (burning inferno of desire).

After you have rated your passion for these activities, make it a priority to pursue those that have a rating of four or five. Anything less than a four is not something that will excite you enough to motivate you to pursue it with gusto.

With passion as the driving force, you won't have to force yourself to get involved in these activities. If anything, you will have to force yourself not to get involved in these activities. Passion, enthusiasm, and desire are what you need to get yourself into activities that will give you the most satisfaction and fulfillment. When you are more motivated to do those challenging activities, you can't help but learn and grow as a person.

Answer to Exercise 8-1: Make sure the television isn't plugged in while you pursue more rewarding activities in front of it.

CHAPTER 9

Zen There Was the Now

Now and Only Now You Have the Now

Out of 500 people surveyed by *World Tennis Magazine* in a sex/tennis poll, 54 percent of the respondents said they think about sex while playing tennis. So what does this mean? It could mean a number of things: Possibly they find tennis boring. Maybe they are playing with, or against, some pretty sexy partners. How about a Freudian explanation? They are so obsessed about sex that they think about it all the time, whether they are playing tennis, eating a meal, sewing a dress, or riding a horse.

My stab at an explanation simply states that these tennis players just have a hard time living in the moment. They can't be present, no matter what they are doing. The magazine didn't poll the respondents on this, but I would imagine some of these same people think about tennis while having sex. We will leave that poll for *World Sex Magazine* to conduct. It would also be interesting to conduct a poll to find out how many musicians think about sex while playing in a symphony orchestra.

> The day is of infinite length for him who knows how to appreciate and use it.
> —*Johann Wolfgang von Goethe*

Like the tennis players, most of us don't live the "now." We live either the "before," or the "then," in place of the "now." Many of life's most precious moments are missed because we are so preoccupied with

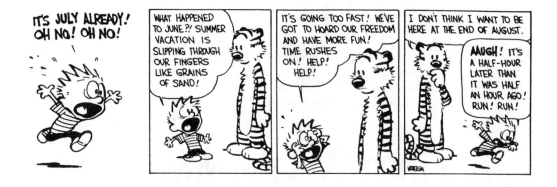

either the past or the future. The notion of living in the now isn't an overly profound idea; yet few of us do it.

Most of us walk around the majority of the time as if we were sleeping, paying little attention to what is going on around us. Some philosophers say most of us are unconscious most of the time.

If you want to be one of the conscious minority, remember now—and only now—you have the now. Being in the now is important because this moment is all you really have. There is nothing you can ever experience, except the present moment. Being in the now means accepting that you can never experience past or future moments. **This is it!** Believe it or not, now is all you will ever get in life.

Mastering the Moment

In some cultures, a moment can last the entire afternoon. Activities have natural starting and ending times not dictated by the clock. A conversation with another person isn't dependent on a limited time of fifteen or thirty minutes; it starts when it starts and ends when it ends. Unfortunately, many North Americans aren't able to have a leisurely talk with any of their relatives, friends, or neighbors. It takes too much unstructured time, with natural starting and ending times.

Lost, yesterday, somewhere between sunrise and sunset, two golden hours, each set with sixty diamond minutes. No reward is offered, for they are gone forever.

—Horace Mann

Being in the now is nothing more than enjoying the present for all it's worth. This is what Mij Relge, a very good friend of mine, has been able to do. At the age of forty-three, Mij quit his job as a university professor to do some soul-searching, and to grow as a person. Out of curiosity, I asked him what he was doing with all his free time and what his plans were for the future. This was after he had been jobless for about two years. Mij responded with a Zen-type answer, indicating he wasn't having any trouble at all with his work-free life. He replied that he was simply "mastering the moment."

Mastering the moment is important for enjoying leisure (and life in general). Quality leisure in your life is dependent on the ability to be totally involved in the activity. Only then can you get full satisfaction from what you are doing. This is true whether you are playing chess, talking to a friend, wading through a stream, or watching a sunset. Spending leisure in the now produces a feeling of vivid attentiveness, as well as a sense of real peace with the world.

Being in the now is emphasized in Zen, an Eastern discipline, which has personal enlightenment as its goal. The following Zen story illustrates the importance of mastering the moment:

A student of Zen asked his teacher, "Master, what is Zen?" The master replied, "Zen is sweeping the floors when you sweep the floors, eating when you eat, and sleeping when you sleep." The student responded by saying, "Master that is so simple." "Of course," said the Master. "But so few people ever do it."

Most people are seldom in the present moment. This is unfortunate since they miss out on many opportunities in life. Having presence of mind, or paying attention to the moment, is something that most of us can improve upon and from which we all can benefit. The ability to be in the now and concentrate on the task at hand is a very important aspect of the creative process for both work and play.

> Time is nature's way of keeping everything from happening at once.
>
> —Unknown Wise Person

Essential to mastering the moment is learning to do one thing at a time, instead of two or three. Doing something physically and thinking about something else at the same time are contradictory. We aren't free to take part in our chosen activities if we are thinking about something else. One of the problems we have with leisure is choosing something and sticking with it until it is time to quit. Any act or task should be worthy of our total attention, if it is worth doing at all.

The ability to experience the here and now is a characteristic of creatively alive individuals. Creatively alive people are those who can get totally immersed in a project. Their concentration level is so high that they lose all sense of time. Their projects totally envelop them—having distracting thoughts isn't a problem. Their secret? They enjoy the moment for what it is and don't worry about what is coming up next.

Have you ever been possessed by energy that carried you away from your normal concerns into a state of optimal satisfaction? If you have, you were mastering the moment and may have experienced numerous feelings that you normally don't experience. Two professors of psychology at Southern Illinois University, Howard E.A. Tinsley and Diane J. Tinsley, found individuals experiencing leisure to the fullest felt the following:

- ➤ A feeling of freedom
- ➤ Total absorption in the activity at hand
- ➤ Lack of focus on self
- ➤ Enhanced perception of objects and events
- ➤ Little awareness of the passage of time
- ➤ Increased sensitivity to body sensations
- ➤ Increased sensitivity to emotions

Cam Gase from San Diego, California, sent me the following letter. Cam is obviously someone who enjoys the moment.

Dear Ernie,

I really enjoyed your book. I read it while on "watch" last night, midnight to eight AM. I am an able seaman on a ship in the Indian Ocean now anchored in a lagoon. As I came across the idea of enjoying sunsets and full moons, I was looking at a full moon, then shortly thereafter a beautiful sunrise. I guess leisurely people don't get up for sunrises. We are on the same wavelength. I self-published a small book of quotations, and I see many of them in your book.

Being a seaman, I enjoy and do a lot of traveling. A few years ago I took my girlfriend to Hong Kong and Bangkok. Then last year we went to London, Amsterdam, Munich, Venice, Switzerland, and Paris. We are going on a Caribbean cruise in January.

People working on these ships work hard seven days a week—especially holidays and weekends due to the higher pay. Anyway, I took the day off and went to the beach to go swimming and write a few letters. People were astounded that I would loaf on a "premium pay" day. Tomorrow is Sunday, and I'm going to do the same. I have so many things to do in my leisure time: read, write, swim, etc. I don't watch TV, but I do watch some videos and films.

Your concept of living like you had six months left is one I picked up while studying Ninja philosophy and art. Living in the now is described as "Being there: totally concentrating on the moment at hand." Yoga and Zen training used the idea of concentrating on a simple object as you described.

I truly enjoy my solitude too. It's just great when I read a book and agree with every page. I am surprised that someone put all the ideas and concepts in one book.

Sincerely,

Cam

Cam knows that the secret to being happy at leisure is to frequently participate in activities in which he can master the moment. If you can do the same, you will be carried away by experiences that are extraordinarily joyous, fulfilling, and meaningful. Mastering the moment is spending an afternoon browsing without a definite purpose in a library or writing a letter by hand that flows on with endless ideas. It is the experience of doing something with so much fascination and enjoyment that you lose all sense of time and place. When you are mastering the moment, nothing is important, except what you are doing at that time.

Must be nice to cruise around in a Porsche.

Must be nice to just goof off for the afternoon.

Time Is Happiness

> If you're not served in 5 minutes
> you'll get served in 8 or 9…
> Maybe 12 minutes
> RELAX!
>
> —*On menu of Ritz Diner, Edmonton*

Many people are in a mad rush to get somewhere, but it's quite apparent they don't have the slightest notion why they are in such a hurry or, even worse, where they are going. They appear to be in a hurry to get to a destination, so they can arrive quicker and wait longer.

What is your hurry in life? When was the last time you had a heart-to-heart conversation with a friend? Have you ever stopped to consider why you are rushing around? Do you rush to the phone when there is no need to do so? You can allow it to ring another ring without anything serious happening.

Nothing is so dear and precious as time.
—French Proverb

People suffering from "hurry sickness" tend to have many health problems, including a high mortality rate from heart disease. Physiological characteristics of people consumed by time include increased heart rate, high blood pressure, gastric problems, and muscle tension. In a rush to do it all, time-driven people can develop serious illnesses that lead to early deaths.

The following list gives you some ways to slow down and enjoy life:

➤ Don't be immersed in the future. Stop worrying about things you have to do and whether you have time for them. If you have the time, you will complete tasks. If you don't have enough time, you can complete the tasks tomorrow.

➤ When you have a cup of coffee, live the moment. Drink the coffee slowly and with great concentration, as if the whole world had stopped to help you enjoy the coffee.

➤ Quit speeding in your car. Slow down even if you are in a hurry.

➤ Have thirty minutes or so of unstructured time every day to do something spontaneous and different.

➤ Spend time alone for an hour or two every day and let the telephone answering machine take your calls.

➤ Truly watch a sunset in the evening for the amount of time it takes to have the sun go down.

➤ Have a real conversation with your neighbor during which you have a natural starting time and finishing time not dictated by the clock.

➤ Experience your shower in the morning for as long as it takes you to truly experience it.

In a culture addicted to materialism, workaholism, and speed, the battle cry is: "Time is money." I say the heck with time measured in terms of money. I choose to value my time in terms of happiness. Let the motto "time is happiness" replace "time is money" and we will all be healthier and better off.

Ultimately Nothing Matters and So What if It Did

Worrying about the trivial or the important is one of the activities that robs people of the now. About 15 percent of the U.S. public spends at least 50 percent of each day worrying, says a study from Pennsylvania State University. Worry is so rampant in North America that certain researchers claim approximately one out of three people in North American society has serious mental problems as a result of worrying. On that note, think of two of your friends. If you consider both of them mentally healthy, then you must be the one out of the three with the mental problems (I'm just kidding).

> I am an old man and have known a great many troubles, but most of them never happened.
> —Mark Twain

Exercise 9-1. Two Days About Which Not to Worry

There are two days of the week about which you should not worry. What are these two days?

To put worrying in proper perspective, here is another story told in Zen teachings:

> Two monks, Eanzan and Tekido, were walking along a muddy road when they came upon a beautiful woman who was unable to cross the road without getting her silk shoes muddy. Without saying a word, Eanzan picked up the woman and carried her across the road, leaving her on the other side. Then the two monks continued walking without talking until the end of the day. When they reached their destination, Tekido said, "You know monks are supposed to avoid women. Why did you pick up that woman this morning?" Eanzan replied, "I left her on the side of the road. Why are you at this time still carrying her?"

The above story emphasizes the Zen belief in the importance of going through life without carrying around problems from the past. Yet many people focus on former problems. Worrying comprises most of people's thinking; some people are so used to worrying that they worry if they don't have anything to worry about.

If you are a chronic worrier and don't have enough things to worry about, you can use some

> It isn't the experience of today that drives men mad. It is the remorse for something that happened yesterday, and the dread of what tomorrow may disclose.
> —Robert Jones Burdette

items from the following list. I generated this list when I suggested that we have obsession readings at one of my favorite coffee bars instead of the poetry readings some coffee bars have. As with all my great ideas, this idea wasn't welcomed with open arms.

Some More Things to Worry About

- ➤ What will happen to this world if I get overmotivated?
- ➤ Who keeps stealing my socks?
- ➤ What will I wear if I am invited as a guest on Oprah?
- ➤ Who invented socks?
- ➤ Will someone else be reincarnated as me?
- ➤ How come all the crazy guys at the coffee bar know me?
- ➤ Is my neighbor's cat dysfunctional?
- ➤ Why didn't Celine Dion marry me instead?
- ➤ What type of car should I buy if I win the lottery?
- ➤ Why am I the only customer in this coffee shop?
- ➤ How many rebuses have been created?
- ➤ Am I so smart that I am wasting my life no matter what I do?
- ➤ Do dyslexics appreciate palindromes?
- ➤ Is my purpose in life to be a warning for others?
- ➤ Who is that beautiful blond over there?
- ➤ Do I actually have more fun with blonds?
- ➤ If I marry a blond, will I end up liking brunettes more?
- ➤ Why don't people put fender skirts on cars anymore?
- ➤ Can a perfectionist like me have a paradigm shift?
- ➤ Am I the only one who hasn't had a paradigm shift?
- ➤ Will someone steal this list and sell it to David Letterman for a big fortune?
- ➤ Will they lock me up for having prepared this list?

The world is ruled by letting things take their course. It cannot be ruled by interfering.

—Lao-tzu

Fear, anxiety, and guilt are emotions related to worrying. At any given time, at work or elsewhere, people's minds are far, far away—mostly thinking about worries and regrets. Most people are worrying about what happened yesterday or what will happen tomorrow. This leads to the answer for Exercise 9-1: The two days of the week about which you should not worry are tomorrow and yesterday.

Are you spending too much time worrying and missing out on today?

Can you concentrate and be in the here and now? Spending too much time worrying about losing, failing, or making mistakes will make you tense and anxious. Too much worrying predisposes you to stress, headaches, panic attacks, ulcers, and other related ailments. Most worry is self-inflicted and somewhat useless. Just consider the following chart:

Wasted Worries

40 percent of worries are about events that will never happen
30 percent of worries are about events that already happened
22 percent of worries are about trivial events
4 percent of worries are about events we cannot change
4 percent of worries are about real events on which we can act

---

The above chart indicates that 96 percent of the energy we spend on worrying is used on things we cannot control. This signifies that 96 percent of our worrying is wasted time. In fact, it is even worse than that. Worry about things we can control is wasted as well, since we can control these things. In other words, worry about things we can't control is wasted because we can't control them, and worry about things we can control is wasted because we can control these things. The result is 100 percent of our worrying is wasted. (Now you can worry about all the time you have been wasting while worrying.)

> Half of our life is spent trying to find something to do with the time we have rushed through life trying to save.
> —Will Rogers

Spending time worrying about past events or future concerns is a waste of energy. Creative people realize Murphy's Law has some bearing on the way things will be; that is, "If anything can go wrong, it will."

Hurdles are a certainty in life. There is no way for the highly creative to eliminate all the hurdles. Many new hurdles will appear regularly, but creative people realize there is a way to overcome virtually all hurdles.

When a hurdle appears, creative people will figure out a way to eliminate the hurdle. If they can't get over it, they will go under it. If they can't get under it, they will go around it. If they can't go around it, they will go through it. With all these options, there is no need to worry about hurdles, only whether or not there is a hurdle now. If there isn't one, fine. If there is one, fine again, because there is a challenge to face and a new problem to solve.

Most, if not all, worrying robs you of energy that can be channeled into solving problems. Here is a good attitude for you to adopt: Ultimately nothing matters, and so what if it did? If you can live this motto, most of your worries will be eliminated.

Giving Up Control to Be in Control

Many people want to be in total control at all times. They worry and are insecure when they feel out of control. The need for control can be self-defeating. The creatively alive people of this world say one important factor for being fully alive is having the ability to yield or give up the need to control. Of course, this goes against what we have allowed ourselves to believe.

When you have got an elephant by the hind leg, and he is trying to run away, it's best to let him run.

—Abraham Lincoln

If you have ever ridden a horse, you realize it is much easier to ride a horse in the direction it wants to go. Getting through life in this world is also easier if you ride with the world in the direction it's going. This means giving up the need to control the way everything is going to turn out. To illustrate the importance of giving up control in life, I find it useful to use this analogy:

Assume you are on a raft floating down a fast moving and highly treacherous river. The raft happens to capsize, and you fall into the rapidly flowing water. There are two things you can do. One is to try and take control and fight the river. If you do this, you are liable to end up injured as a result of being thrown against the rocks. The second thing you can do is give up total control. The moment you give up control you will be in control. You are now going with the flow. The water doesn't go into the rocks; the water goes around the rocks.

Life is a fast moving river. To get through life with a minimum of scrapes and bruises, we must learn how to go with the flow. Going with the flow means giving up control. It means surrendering to the notion that we don't know how anything is going to turn out. The best way to be in control of our destinies is to give up control and not worry about how things are going to turn out. Too many factors beyond our control will destroy the best of plans.

Creatively alive people yield and go with the flow. In going with the flow, creatively alive people are acknowledging the importance of mastering the moment.

Don't Plan to Be Spontaneous

Unlike the majority of adults, creatively alive adults live the moment. Similarly, unlike the majority of adults, creatively alive adults can be spontaneous. I think Mark Twain was probably speaking of his lack of spontaneity as an adult when he said, "It usually takes me more than three weeks to prepare a good impromptu speech."

Abraham Maslow, the famous humanist psychologist, believed spontaneity is a trait that is too often lost as people grow older. Maslow said, "Almost any child can compose a song or poem or a dance or a painting or a play or a game on the spur of the moment, without planning or previous intent." The majority of adults lose this ability, according to Maslow. Nevertheless, Maslow found a small fraction of adults didn't lose this trait or regained it later in life. These are the people who are self-actualized. Recall from Chapter 7 that self-actualization is the state of outstanding mental

I had planned to be spontaneous today at three o'clock, but I'm swamped. It looks like I'll have to reschedule it for tomorrow.

health. Maslow called this a state of being fully human. He found self-actualized people to be spontaneous and highly creative in their journey towards maturity.

Spontaneity is, essentially, synonymous with creative living. Creatively alive people aren't inhibited; they can express their true feelings. They are able, like children, to play and act foolish. They also are able, on the spur of the moment, to do something not in their plans for that day. Creative people also have no problem with impromptu speeches. They are more like children when they speak, rather than like adults.

How spontaneous are you? Do you always stick to your plans for the day? Do you always follow a set routine? How often do you ignore your plans and do something different? I have found that when I do something spontaneous, unexpected and interesting things happen to me. Many times I wind up with rewarding experiences that I would have never achieved by sticking to my plans.

Watch children to refresh your notion of spontaneity. If you can be a child again, you can be spontaneous. Being spontaneous means challenging your plans; it means being able to try something new on the spur of the moment because it may be something you will enjoy. Although most accountants and engineers would probably try to plan to be more spontaneous, no one can plan spontaneity. "Planned spontaneity" is an oxymoron.

Being spontaneous also means allowing more chance in your life. The more chance you let in your world, the more interesting your world of leisure will become. Let more people in your life. Communicate with them and express yourself to them, especially if they have different viewpoints from your own. You might learn something new.

Remember to be spontaneous on a regular basis. Every day practice doing something that you haven't planned. On the spur of the moment, choose and do something new and exciting. It can be quite a small thing, like taking a different route somewhere, eating in a different restaurant, or going to some new kind of entertainment. You can make your life of leisure much more interesting by introducing something novel in all your activities.

Living Happily Ever After on a Day-to-Day Basis

Some time ago, I encountered a semi-derelict walking out of a third-rate hotel in the morning. There wasn't anyone with him at the time, and he was unaware of my presence. I overheard him say with great joy and enthusiasm, "Good morning world, how are you?" Then he looked at the surroundings and the bright sun, and said with a glow in his face, "Amazing, just amazing!"

I was in awe of this man. He was able to show great joy, although he didn't seem to have the many other material things people strive for in our society. When I saw how happy he was to be alive, I was surprised he wasn't levitating. Then I thought about the thousands of miserable faces I would have seen if I had been downtown that morning. It would have been difficult for me to find one employed person showing so much joy, just for being alive that day. The faces I would have encountered would have displayed the seriousness normally seen on the faces of musicians playing in a symphony orchestra. And I am sure if I was to hear their conversations, most wouldn't have been about happy events.

We have no more right to consume happiness without producing it, than to consume wealth without producing it.
—George Bernard Shaw

Abraham Lincoln said most folks are about as happy as they make up their minds to be. I am sure the semi-derilect whom I encountered that morning would have said the same thing. So there you have it folks;

you're about as happy as you want to be. For centuries, great thinkers and religious leaders from different faiths have been saying basically the same thing about happiness. They could shout it from the rooftops and cast it in every stone; most people still won't get it. Happiness is on the inside, not on the outside. True happiness is finding contentment within oneself. All the possessions in the world aren't going to bring anyone the happiness that some people with virtually no possessions experience from within.

One common goal in life is to be happy. Just like the fictitious characters we read about in fairy tales when we were children, most people would like to live happily ever after. They want to have nothing but good times.

Life can only be lived happily ever after on a day-to-day basis. Happiness is something that happens in the now. If your primary goal in life is to be happy, happiness will elude you. Happiness is a product of achieving goals, but not a goal in itself.

My goals in life are to be happy, live every moment for all it's worth, and learn to do one thing at a time.

Having as many good times as possible is another unsatisfactory goal. Pleasure or having good times is normally just an escape from the experience of discomfort. Too much pleasure in itself can become very dull. If life was all pleasure and nothing else, there would be no happiness.

Happiness has to do with being engaged. This is true in the workplace; this is also true away from the workplace. Being engaged literally means being totally immersed in any task. It means doing just one thing at a time, and enjoying it for all it's worth.

As they say in Zen, if you can't find it where you're standing, where do you expect to wander in search of it? The great minds of Eastern philosophy have always said, "Happiness is the way." What they have been saying is happiness is not a destination. It is nothing you look for; you create it. You don't have to go looking for happiness—if that's where you're coming from.

The time to relax is when you don't have time for it.
—Sydney J. Harris

Humor Is No Laughing Matter

The ability to laugh is a great asset for living life to the fullest. Most people think they possess a sense of humor, but few show it. The seriousness of some people I have met is enough to run trains off their rails.

George Burns felt he would live to be a hundred. In his early nineties, he started taking bookings for his hundredth birthday. Burns lived as long as he did partly because of the attitude he carried throughout his life. He made a living out of humor. Undoubtedly, his health benefited from his work. Researchers are finding that boisterous laughing many times a day will give you the same effects on your health as a ten-mile run.

> The most wasted day of all is that on which we have not laughed.
> —Sébastian Roch Nicolas Chamfort

Another man who benefited from laughter was Norman Cousins. Faced with what doctors diagnosed as a terminal illness, Cousins proved the medics wrong by watching reruns of *Candid Camera* and Groucho Marx films. He was able to laugh himself back to health.

Besides being beneficial to our health, humor is an effective way for promoting creativity. Experts in creativity have observed that stunning solutions are often triggered by humor. Seriousness hinders the creative flow. When you are under a lot of stress and pressure or stuck in a serious state of mind, the best thing to do is to get out a joke book. Get together with someone who can laugh about anything. Fool around. You'll be surprised at the many creative ideas that start to flow.

People who never get carried away should be. Most people have heard the saying "Life is much too important to be taken seriously." Yet how many pay heed to this? Most are too serious. How serious are you in life? Do you find time to laugh, play, and be foolish? If you are always serious and trying to be reasonable, you are sabotaging your creativity. Individuals who are too serious to have fun rarely come up with new and stunning ideas about how to live life.

> Seriousness is the only refuge of the shallow.
> —Oscar Wilde

Play is at the heart of being creatively alive. Playing and having fun are great ways to stimulate our minds. When we are having fun, we tend to be relaxed and enthusiastic. Sometimes we even become outrageous. All these states complement the creative spirit.

Do you ever wonder why children are so creative? Children know how to be spontaneous, how to play, and how to have fun. Remember when you were a child. When you were playing, you were learning. You probably learned more during your lighter moments than during your serious moments. Try and re-experience the child in you if you want to increase your creativity. Keep the child in you alive and don't lose touch with the craziness in you. This will assure that your life will never be boring.

Comedy and laughing will open up your thinking. Laughing tends to make us look at things in unusual ways because laughter changes our state of mind. In a relaxed state, our minds show little concern for being wrong or being practical. It is okay to be foolish; this fosters the flow of creative solutions. Creativity requires both playfulness and foolishness. These are the things society discourages. You may be told to "grow up," but you should never "grow up," because if you do, you will have stopped growing as an individual. If you are the serious type, learn to lighten up. As a friend once told me, "It is impossible to overestimate the unimportance of nearly everything."

The Ultimate Goal Is the Process

Free time is not automatically rewarding. To create satisfaction in our lives, we must put in some effort and attain some accomplishment. If we want to achieve something significant, we must get the ball, get it rolling, and keep it rolling.

The happiest people in life don't look for outside influences to make them happy. They take action and make things happen. The doers of this world aren't content to just drift aimlessly and let life happen to them. They set goals and then take steps to attain them. Once goals are set, working towards the goals is more important than attaining the goals.

The road is better than the inn.
—Miguel de Cervantes

Leo Tolstoy asked three questions:

1. When is the best time to heed? Now.
2. Who are the most esteemed people? He with whom you are.
3. What important pursuits are to be undertaken first? That which does good to him.

When Leo Tolstoy answered these questions, he was reinforcing the power of being in the now. He was underscoring the importance of focusing on the process at hand and not the end result. By focusing on the process, we get to enjoy both the process and the end result.

Living in the moment means there is more enjoyment and satisfaction from our efforts than from actually reaching the goal. Satisfaction from reaching a goal, no matter how significant the goal, is short-lived. Robert Louis Stevenson said, "To travel hopefully is a better thing than to arrive." When the ultimate goal becomes the process, life is transformed. Creativity flows more readily, failure is viewed as success, and losing means winning; the journey becomes the destination.

If you want to travel a happy journey, learn to cultivate a higher appreciation for what is around you—sunsets, music, and other wonderful things. Don't take things for granted, because you'll miss life. Keep in mind that every sunset is different from all other sunsets, just like every snowflake is different from all other snowflakes. Wake up and listen to the birds singing, smell the flowers, and feel the texture of the trees.

Try to find something to enjoy every minute of the day. Look for the positive in all situations. Start and live each day with a task in mind. In your field of consciousness, practice the idea of enjoying your day. Act with a presence of mind and experience each moment by being in the now. Remember that there is no other moment than this one; you can live only one moment at a time. Ultimately you are the moment.

CHAPTER 10

It Is Better to Be Alone than in Bad Company

The Key to Being Alone Is Locked Inside

The Maytag man in television commercials is depicted as a lonely repairman. His services aren't required very often because of the high quality of the Maytag appliances he is supposed to service. In one commercial the Maytag man registers at a hotel and signs his company name at the desk. The receptionist says something like, "We'll try to make sure you're not lonely here." In real life the receptionist would be fooling herself. No one can ever ensure the Maytag man isn't lonely except the Maytag man himself. Furthermore, just because the Maytag man spends substantial time alone, he doesn't have to be lonely.

> *A man who finds no satisfaction in himself, seeks for it in vain elsewhere.*
>
> —*François, Duc de La Rochefoucauld*

There are two sides to being alone: The painful side is loneliness. The other side to being alone is the pleasant side, solitude. Discovering solitude means discovering many delightful activities that can only be enjoyed alone. Unfortunately, most people never discover the pleasant side to being alone.

To most people, being alone means experiencing loneliness. I know people who can be driven off their rails if they are forced to be alone for more than ten minutes. Whenever these individuals wind up alone, they are immediately lonely.

Lonely people use aloneness as an excuse for not being able to do anything enjoyable in their spare time. I have a friend who was enthusiastic about cycling one summer. He bought a bicycle and then used it only once in the first two months. He wouldn't go cycling because he had no one with whom to cycle. I feel sorry for him because he is missing out on great opportunities for enjoying his leisure. I often insist on going cycling or jogging alone, even when one or two friends are around and want to come along. Of course, I have to convince my friends that I don't find their company boring. I am merely looking for some solitude, which I treasure immensely. There are times when I prefer the pleasure I get from my own company.

> City Life: Millions of people being lonesome together.
> —Henry David Thoreau

I know other people who will put on the television or radio the minute they are alone. They will watch boring television programs or listen to radio deejays engage in idle chatter rather than deal with periods of silence. Many people remain in completely unfulfilled relationships rather than risk being alone.

It is most unfortunate that being alone is looked upon as antisocial behavior. Influenced by social programming, most people learn early in life to spend all their leisure time with planned social activities. They join clubs, teams, and any other organizations that will ensure they are with someone. If they wind up alone, with unscheduled time, on a long weekend, they are totally lost.

Psychologists say loneliness has become a serious problem in North America, especially in big cities. Surveys indicate one quarter of the population suffers from chronic loneliness. To some, loneliness is so painful they commit suicide. The following are some reasons people give for their loneliness:

- ➤ Not enough friends
- ➤ Not being married
- ➤ Not having a relationship
- ➤ Living in a new city
- ➤ Living in a big city
- ➤ Superficial friends

Loneliness is even more tragic when you consider that no item in the above list ultimately causes loneliness. These may be influences, but they don't cause loneliness. People are lonely because they allow themselves to get lonely. Loneliness reflects boredom.

To overcome boredom, we must learn how to spend our time alone in a creative manner. The majority of us flee to society—as dull as society is—searching for some excitement to escape the greater dullness inside us. We also flee to society because we fear being alone. We feel we can avoid loneliness by being with people. However, we can be lonelier in a crowd than when we are alone.

Loneliness isn't synonymous with aloneness. The inability to be alone reflects some basic inner insecurity. Some of the loneliest people in the world are people who are always around other people. Many lonely people are extremely charming; they also appear to be self-confident and have great composure. Nevertheless, they are prone to loneliness the minute they are by themselves. Because of a lack of inner security, these people spend every possible minute with other people.

Most people don't want to look inside themselves. Some take drugs or alcohol to keep the pace moving fast. Others—so they don't have to think—turn on the television

If this is loneliness, I want more of it.

or play the stereo to ensure there is always some sound during the times they are alone. The Sufi religious sect has a parable relating the folly of people looking to the external world when one should be looking within. The parable is about their fictitious little man called Mullah:

> One day Mullah is out on the street, outside his house, on his hands and knees looking for something. A friend happens to come by and says, "Mullah, what are you searching for?" Mullah says, "I lost my keys." The friend says, "I'll help you look for them." After some time, the friend finds looking for the keys quite tiresome and says to Mullah, "Mullah, do you have any idea where you lost the keys?" Mullah replies, "Yes, I lost the keys in the house." The bewildered friend then asks Mullah, "Why in the world are we looking for the keys outside?" Mullah answers, "Because there is a lot more light out here."

This parable is funny, but it has a serious side to it. To handle loneliness, most people look to the external world, where there is more light. Just as Mullah won't find his keys outside his house, people who look outside of themselves to overcome loneliness won't find the key to handling loneliness. The key to handling loneliness and being alone is locked inside. Once people recognize what causes their loneliness, being alone becomes an opportunity to do many interesting and enjoyable things that they can't do around other people.

Enjoying Being Alone Takes High Self-esteem

Being afraid to be alone is a sign of low self-esteem. This comes from a sense of feeling unworthy and undeserving. Our lives can feel like one big mess without self-esteem.

Many people are approval-seekers, always trying to get positive feedback from others. Even if it is forthcoming, this doesn't contribute to self-esteem. Esteem from others and self-esteem are two different things. As we saw in Maslow's hierarchy of needs, all of us would like esteem from others as well as from ourselves, but the two esteem needs aren't based on the same foundations.

In life there is no substitute for happiness, and there can be little happiness without self-esteem. Self-esteem cannot be achieved through other people or through the environment; it is something individuals can only give themselves. People with low self-esteem are dependent upon how other people evaluate them. This makes them vulnerable to what others think or say. These other people aren't the best judges, because they, too, probably have low self-esteem and are caught up in trying to get approval from the achievement-oriented and moneymaking external world.

If you can only make it with people, and not alone, you can't make it.

—Clark E. Moustakas

Can you enjoy being alone? If you can't, it is probably a sign that you aren't able to discover quality in your own character. Not liking yourself can be a giant barrier to enjoying solitary leisure time. Incidentally, if you don't like yourself, why would you expect anyone else to like you?

Finding out to what degree you like yourself involves looking at how much effort you put into trying to get others to like you. If you are constantly afraid someone may not like you or may get upset with you, you probably have low self-esteem. On the other hand, if you have high self-esteem, you don't fear having people disagree with you, or even upset with you. As a person with high self-esteem, you undoubtedly have friends with quality and not friends in quantity. There is a big difference

here: Friends in quantity tend to be high in number, but superficial in character. Friends with quality are lower in number, but have greater character.

If you lack self-esteem, you must develop it. It is based on your ability to like yourself no matter what others think about you. You may have to give up certain friends and acquaintances if they aren't supportive during your transition. In doing so, you get to keep your own scorecard based on your own standards, rather than basing your scorecard on someone else's standards.

You must love yourself and the world before you can serve the world. Developing higher self-esteem enables you to escape any rut in which you find yourself. Once you achieve higher self-esteem, you will learn how to accomplish, to achieve, and to triumph when alone. You will get to know yourself; in yourself is the universe.

Don't Just Walk Away from Negative People: Run!

If you possess high self-esteem, you will avoid being around certain people, even if the alternative is being alone. While you are trying to light the fire in your life, learn to ignore people who will try to put it out for you. The boring person we talked about in Chapter 6 may douse your fire somewhat, but negative people are even more dangerous to your happiness and well-being.

Negative people are particularly noted for their lack of humor. They have the delightful view that life is a rip-off and that nothing is so bad that it can't get worse. Negative people will seek your support for their notion that the world is a lousy place. Nothing irks negative and unmotivated people more than individuals who are positive and successful. Especially irritated by other people who are happy and highly motivated, negative people will do anything in their powers to bring positive people down to their depressing level. At social gatherings, these neurotics are the life of the party, when they leave.

You must spot and avoid people who are likely to drain your energy. If you have friends or acquaintances who are constantly depressed and complaining about life, their negative energy will sap your positive energy. Don't spend a great deal of time with a person who has a negative attitude, unless his or her state of mind is temporary, due to some serious problem. It is in your best interests to avoid negative people as much as possible.

Life is much easier if you don't carry excess baggage. Negative people are excess baggage you can't afford to carry. On an airline, excess baggage will cost you money. Negative people will cost you much more than money. The price will be your time, energy, and happiness. Negative people can even cost you your sanity in the end. At best, you won't succeed in your goals and projects—which are important to your happiness and satisfaction—if you surround yourself with too many negative people.

I was going to buy a copy of The Power of Positive Thinking, and then I thought: What the damn good would that do?
—Ronnie Shakes

No doubt you have heard the joke about the drunk who was lying in the gutter where a pig had also stopped to rest. A woman happened to walk by and said: "You can judge one's character by the company one keeps." The pig promptly got up and walked away. Another mistake some individuals make is to hang around with lazy and negative people because they look like geniuses in the eyes of this company. Unfortunately, the rest of the world, like the lady in the joke, judges you by the company you keep.

Surround yourself with enthusiastic people who have positive things to say about life. Enthusiastic people have an inner fire and an incredible zest for living that is irresistible. Their radiance creates an energy field that anyone in the vicinity is sure to feel. You can learn a lot from positive people. They have acquired a great deal of wisdom and knowledge about life. If nothing else, common sense tells us to surround ourselves with highly motivated individuals, instead of people who rob us of our energy.

Don't make the mistake of trying to change negative people, expecting their imminent transformation into more positive individuals. In his book *One*, Richard Bach wrote: "No one can solve problems for someone whose problem is that they don't want problems solved." In case you haven't learned, negative people don't change. If they do, it is only after a lengthy period, time you can't afford to lose. Instead of expending your energy trying to change someone, utilize that energy in changing yourself for the better.

If you are a Good Samaritan, who likes to take on one or two neurotics as a personal project, I must warn you about the futility of this venture. Unless you can get these people to have personality transplants, all your efforts will be in vain. Here is an old tale about a scorpion and a frog to put negative people in the proper perspective:

> A scorpion, wanting to get across a pond, spots a friendly frog. The scorpion says to the frog, "How about a lift to the other side of the pond. I can't swim, and I would appreciate your helping me out."
>
> The frog says, "No way. I know what scorpions are like. If I let you on my back, you'll probably sting me halfway across the pond, from where I could not swim to shore after being stung. I don't want to drown."
>
> The scorpion replies, "Don't be silly. If I am on your back, I am dependent on you to get across the pond. If I sting you, I will drown, too. Why would I want to do that?"
>
> The frog thinks about this and relents. "I guess you're right. Hop on." The scorpion hops on the frog's back and they take off for the other side of the pond. The scorpion resists stinging the frog until they are about halfway across the pond. Then the scorpion who, like most of us, can resist everything but temptation, gives the frog a big whopper of a sting.
>
> As both of them start to go under, the frog says to the scorpion, "Why in the world did you do that? Now both of us are going to die."
>
> The scorpion's answer is one you have heard many times before from human scorpions: "I couldn't resist it. It's my nature to be that way."

The moral of this story is that, even if their happiness and survival are at stake, negative people won't change their nature. Although they can change, negative people go on defending their points of view at all costs. Not only do they bring themselves down with their thinking, they try to bring others down with them. Misery doesn't only love company; it demands it.

In dealing with negative people, remember what George Washington said: "It is better to be alone than in bad company." Based on my experience, I believe there is only one way to effectively deal with negative people: Eliminate them from your life. Avoid negative people for the sake of your happiness. When you find yourself in their company, don't walk away from them: **run**!

I will always cherish the initial misconceptions I had about you.
—Unknown Wise Person

Being Alone in Your Tree

Enjoying being alone means making peace with yourself. If there is a key rule for getting the most from being alone, it is that you have to like and enjoy your own company. Being alone forces you to confront yourself. You will find that being alone allows you to experience the world and yourself in a way not available when you are with other people. You get to fly solo rather than with someone else. By flying solo, you are able to achieve greater heights in your leisure pursuits.

The day you feel lonely you can react in one of two ways: One response is known as sad passivity. This includes crying, moping, excess eating, sleeping, and feeling sorry for yourself. This reaction comes from having undefined goals for solitary activities. Undefined goals will cause you to fly solo too low. The only thing responsible for your loneliness is your inactivity. If you are the one who is inactive, you are the sole cause of your loneliness.

Once in a while you have to take a break and visit yourself.
—Audrey Giorgi

The other response is a creative solitude in which defined plans are used to best handle aloneness. These planned activities can include reading, writing letters, studying, listening to music, working on a hobby, or playing a musical instrument. When you start acting on your plans, you will enhance your identity and develop a sense of security.

Exercise 10-2. Being Alone in Your Tree

Being alone is an opportunity to do the things that are difficult to do around other people. Go back to your leisure tree and add a primary branch for activities you can do alone. Now expand your tree by adding those activities that you can pursue alone.

Here are just a few of the many things you can pursue without having someone by your side. You should add those items that interest you to your leisure tree under the category of "solitary activities."

- ➤ Do some meditating and self-examination.
- ➤ Read books and magazines you haven't been able to read before.
- ➤ Go visit people whom you may not visit when you are with another person.
- ➤ Do something artistic or creative.
- ➤ Try volunteer work.
- ➤ Find time to dream your dreams.
- ➤ Discover a new hobby.
- ➤ Take up people watching.
- ➤ Go to coffee places to meet people.
- ➤ Cycle, jog, or swim.
- ➤ Design a new tool or object.
- ➤ Fix your car.
- ➤ Remodel your house.
- ➤ Go for a walk in the park.
- ➤ Walk in the rain.
- ➤ Take a nap.
- ➤ Write letters.
- ➤ Listen to music.
- ➤ Study.
- ➤ Work on a hobby.
- ➤ Take up gardening.

One of the greatest necessities in America is to discover creative solitude.
—Carl Sandburg

There are many more activities that can be pursued while alone. Overcoming loneliness is dependent upon taking action and getting involved. Inactivity and isolation will lead to boredom and depression. Being alone provides an opportunity to develop your individuality and to create quality in your leisure.

Peace of mind can be found in spending a night in your home and in enjoying the quiet spaces. There is substance to being alone because it makes demands on your capacity to rely on yourself. More responsibility is required when you are alone than when you are with your spouse, family, or friends. Taking responsibility means you are the author of your experiences, regardless of what activity you happen to choose.

It is a good thing, every so often, to separate yourself from people, newspapers, radio, and television for at least a day or two. Even if you don't have to spend much time alone at this time in your life, doing it is good for practice. The same reason applies to taking a sabbatical from work. If you do learn to be alone now, you will be better prepared for solitude in the future if you are forced into it. Changes occur in our lives that alter the friendships and the social structures we are used to. Retirement from work, moving to another city, or the death of someone close to us can force us to spend more time alone. Handling being alone prepares you for the times when you may not have as many people around you.

An Artistic Day to Celebrate Being Alone

Solitude can be a great inspiration to the creative artist, an opportunity for renewal and reflection. Most painters, sculptors, poets, writers, and composers spend most of their time alone because they can be much more creative and get more work done.

One way to get in touch with yourself is by getting in touch with the artist or creator within yourself on a planned Artistic or Creator's Day once a week. Call it whatever you want to call it. This is a special outing during which you celebrate your imagination and your unique interests. It doesn't matter whether you think you lack artistic talent. This weekly routine of taking time for yourself will trigger creative talents that you haven't used for some time or didn't know you had.

Knowing others is wisdom, knowing yourself is Enlightenment.

—Lao-tzu

On this day, once a week, for the next three or four months, you get to be alone to pursue something new you have always wanted to pursue or have previously enjoyed doing but have set aside. It is important that you be alone when you participate in this activity. You don't want to be concerned about criticism from others. This is also a time to enjoy being alone.

If you haven't been using the God-given creative ability you used as a child, rediscovering your creativity will enhance your life. Writing is one way to express your creativity. Write a novel or keep a daily journal in which you write your life story. If writing isn't for you, then try wood carving or restoring an old car. The activity can be something truly artistic, such as painting, sculpturing, or writing. It can also be an activity, such as taking a series of photos, which is considered less artistic by some elitists. Start by listing fifteen things you like doing or have always wanted to pursue. Your list may include some of the following activities:

> Write a book.
> Paint a series of pictures.
> Critique ten movies.
> Explore all the interesting sights in your area.
> Write a number of songs.
> Photograph all the species of birds in your area.
> Visit a variety of restaurants to discover the diversity of available meals in your city.
> Attend and critique symphony, opera, and live theater performances.
> Learn to play a musical instrument.

Once you have developed your list, choose some interest to pursue with focus, purpose, and concentration. You must stick to this activity for at least twelve weeks. For twelve weeks or more, you get to be the artist or creator. It is important, on your creative day, to celebrate the process and not the outcome. For example, if you have chosen to write a book, it doesn't matter if the book gets published. The process of writing the book is important because you are actually writing it, instead of just thinking about it.

Once you start writing the book or painting your pictures, you will start to discover your creativity. You will also get to appreciate being alone. Your Artist's or Creator's Day will connect you with your creativity, which you have always had, but suppressed. You will discover you are much more creative than you thought you were.

Solitude makes us tougher towards ourselves and tenderer towards others: in both ways it improves our character.
—Friedrich Nietzsche

When you eventually finish your project, you will experience a great deal of satisfaction and self-confidence. Now, you can also celebrate the outcome. If you chose to write a book, you can now take a risk and show it to friends or relatives. If you chose to paint a series of pictures, so what if someone thinks that they look like the bottom of Lake Superior? Regardless of what people have to say, you will feel an incredible sense of accomplishment from completing your project. You will have seen creative qualities in yourself that you didn't see before. Taking the time to do something imaginative and showing the commitment to take the time for yourself on a regular basis will help you to develop more confidence and courage to happily spend time alone.

Give Solitude a Chance

Many individuals, when confronted with being alone, don't give solitude a chance. They immediately turn on the television or spontaneously decide to go shopping for something that they don't need or can't afford. Because they don't give solitude a chance, they never get to appreciate it.

The great misfortune—to be incapable of solitude.
—Jean de la Bruyère

After having been with people for any length of time, we get addicted to having someone around us, especially when we are with quality people. Richard Bach, in his book *Illusions*, related how it always took some effort and adjustment to return to being by himself after having been around people for some time. He wrote: "Lonely again. A person gets used to being alone, but break it just for a day and you have to get used to it again."

While writing this book, as well as my previous one, I had to get used to being alone. For the first fifteen minutes or half hour, I tended to make phone calls, turn on the radio to a talk show, or read material that had absolutely no use for my projects. I had to first confront the reality that I was alone. Then, I settled into writing and actually enjoyed being alone.

When you find yourself alone, don't try to escape it at the first sign of anxiety or fear. You don't have to feel abandoned or disconnected. Rather than thinking of yourself as being without someone, realize that you are in the company of someone really important—yourself. This is a precious opportunity to pursue the rewards that only dynamic solitude has to offer.

We all experience at least a touch of loneliness at some stage in our lives. Even the most successful individuals, whether single or attached, will experience short periods of loneliness. Individuals who are often alone but don't experience much loneliness feel good about themselves and their lives. They enjoy their own company as much as anyone else's. They also know that satisfaction and happiness in life are possible without an intimate relationship.

When I am alone with all my conveniences, such as the telephone, radio, books, computer, magazines, and various forms of transportation, I may feel just a little lonely for a short period of time. But, I remember that highly motivated individuals have experienced long periods of solitary confinement without feeling their lives were meaningless. The true story of Sidney Rittenberg is enough to put my being alone in proper perspective.

Sidney Rittenberg spent eleven years in a Chinese jail, all in solitary confinement. For years, the guards wouldn't even allow Rittenberg to talk to himself; he also wasn't allowed to have a pen and paper to write letters. He said that he kept reminding himself he could be in downtown New York, among 10,000 people, and be lonelier than he was in jail all those years. If Sidney Rittenberg can spend eleven years in solitary confinement without any conveniences, and come out of it well balanced, certainly the rest of us can deal with being alone a few hours a day.

> Conversation enriches the understanding, but solitude is the school of genius.
> —Edward Gibbon

Sidney Rittenberg made the choice to be happy in his own company; you can do the same. If you are single, possibly the art of loving being alone is the key to being a happy individual, as well as the key to meeting someone special down the road. Being happy alone indicates a strong sense of self, which other well-balanced people find appealing.

Solitude Is for the Sophisticated

To truly experience the joy of not working, you must learn how to appreciate your time alone. Time alone is an opportunity to learn and grow as a person. Being alone is also the time to unplug from the hectic pace of life. The Hindus have a powerful proverb: "You grow only when you are alone." You need time alone as an opportunity to get to know yourself better. Solitude is for thinking through those philosophical issues that affect your life.

Although loneliness can mean dejection and sadness, solitude can mean contentment and even ecstasy. Being alone and happy to be that way represents solitude. Sophisticated or self-actualized personalities treasure solitude. Self-actualized people are at the highest level of self-development and don't flee from aloneness; they seek it. In many of their leisure activities, these people are at their best and most effective when alone. The self-

Great! All the other leaves are gone. Now I can enjoy some solitude.

actualized are centered—meaning they receive a great amount of satis-faction from inside themselves, because they appreciate solitude more than most people.

Self-actualized individuals aren't loners. Loners don't get along with anyone; they are neurotic, secretive, and poorly adjusted psychologi-cally. In contrast, self-actualized individuals are healthy individuals who get along with people. Abraham Maslow, the well-known humanist psy-chologist, found that these psychologically healthy individuals are high-ly independent, yet at the same time they enjoy people.

The paradox is that the people who are self-actualized appear to be loners, but though they may appear to be loners, they actually like to be with people and can be the most sociable people around. They are the most individualist members in society and, at the same time, are the most social, friendly, and loving. They have the ability to get along with others and the ability to get along with themselves. These self-directed people are free from the need to impress others or to be liked by them.

These creatively alive people have developed their natural ability, the ability that gives them the power to be happy in life. Because they have learned how to be independent, they have the ability to work alone and to play alone. Self-actualized people don't base their identities on mem-berships in social groups. They can stand alone in their convictions and desires, often against the opinions and objections coming from others.

While self-actualized people enjoy the presence of others, they don't always need other people. Honors, prestige, and rewards aren't as important for the mentally healthy. Because they aren't as dependent on other people, they require less praise and affection.

If you ever want to experience self-actualization, it is imperative you enjoy being alone. Being self-actualized means you know that the quality in your inner life determines the quality in your external life. Your self-development and movement toward self-actualization can be won-drous, mysterious, and fascinating. Especially when you start spending substantial time alone, you will find a spiritual side to leisure. Quiet spaces will offer opportunity to reflect, to meditate, and to grow; you will find that Nirvana can be found in your own mind.

CHAPTER 11

Being an Aristocrat on Less than Twenty Dollars a Day

Put Money in Its Place

This chapter is about money and what role money should play in our enjoyment of leisure time. Money plays a role, but not as big a role as the majority in our society believes.

Two types of individuals are continually obsessed with money: those who have a lot of it and those who don't have a lot of it. When money is involved, common sense seems to go flying out the window. Psychologists have found that many people have more hang-ups about money than they do about sex. Considering all the financial problems human beings have, it would be better if we didn't have to play the money game.

> *Too many people are thinking of security instead of opportunity. They seem more afraid of life than death.*
>
> *—James F. Byrnes*

Unfortunately, regardless of how much money we have, we all have to play the money game to some extent. Food, housing, education, transportation, health care, and clothing are all based on having adequate money. Most of us have to expend time, energy, and effort to make a living. This interferes with our enjoyment of the really interesting things that life has to offer.

In North America, money shouldn't be the big problem most people make it out to be. The money game is actually quite easy to play if you know the secret that was passed on to me some time ago. There are two powerful ways of handling money. If you don't know the secret, I will share it with you later in this chapter.

My riches consist not in the extent of my possessions but in the fewness of my wants.
—J. Brotherton

Individuals who are satisfying their basic needs in life can alleviate their financial problems by putting the concept of money in its place. Our socioeconomic problems have more to do with values and expectations than with problems with the economy. Most of us can already meet our genuine material needs. We don't have the time to enjoy what we have, and we want more. In all probability, if we presently don't have time to enjoy what we already have, we couldn't find the time to enjoy more things.

The chase after money and material goods is a misdirected effort to make up for what is missing in our lives. This chase undermines some of the things that we already have, such as our relationships. The problem is we judge ourselves by what we can show for our money. By working harder to accumulate more consumer goods, we end up with less time for leisure activities. The chase after money and material goods is normally a disguised chase after something else.

When Enough Is Never Enough

A few years ago, the *Wall Street Journal* commissioned the Roper Organization to see how U.S. citizens defined the American Dream, and whether the Dream was attainable. At one time, the American Dream represented liberty. Now, to most people, the American Dream signifies prosperity or being well-off. People feel free insofar as they have access to money.

Few rich men own their property. Their property owns them.
—Robert G. Ingersoll

Reasonable people would guess that a much higher percentage of affluent people said that they were living the American Dream than those who weren't well-off. This wasn't so. Only 6 percent of those earning $50,000 or more a year said they had attained the Dream as compared to 5 percent of people earning $15,000 a year or less. Those with incomes of $15,000 a year or less felt that the American Dream could be attained with a median income of $50,000 a year, while those with incomes of $50,000 or more felt that it would take at least $100,000 a year to live the Dream.

Economic growth won't bring more happiness to most middle-class North Americans. What are classified as economic problems are really psychological problems in disguise. The well-being of North Americans is suffering both emotionally and physically because of the lack of rich human relations and the lack of time to enjoy what they already have. Well-off individuals often drive themselves to extreme sickness—even death—in the quest for more money. Many people feel empty and deprived after they have achieved great financial success.

In Canada and the United States, the poverty line is now drawn at a level which would be considered that of the middle-class or upper-class in many third-world countries. At one time, owning just a black-and-white TV set was a luxury for the North American middle class. Then, a color set was a luxury. Now, a color set is considered a necessity of life; practically all families below the poverty line own one. Today, if you own two color sets, you probably aren't considered well-off, considering that almost 50 percent of North American households own two or more color television sets.

In 1957, Americans reported the highest level of satisfaction with their lives ever reported. The level of satisfaction in the 1980s and 1990s was significantly lower, despite the fact that the number of American households that own dishwashers has gone up sevenfold and the percentage of households that own two or more cars has tripled. In the 1990s, the average North American owns and consumes twice as much as the average North American did in the 1950s. Nevertheless, the average North American probably complains twice as much in the 1990s as the average North American of the 1950s.

> If I keep my good character,
> I shall be rich enough.
> —Platonicus

The problem is one of greed; most people want to have it all: a lot of money, a big house, two or three cars, and increasingly exotic vacations in the Caribbean and the Orient. This have-it-all mentality has led to a lower degree of satisfaction, even though people today have more than people of any other generation.

We have been programmed to believe that the best material comforts are necessary for happiness. In the United States and Canada, like most affluent Western societies, the majority of us are protected from extreme poverty, hunger, disease, and natural catastrophes to a degree that people in previous generations couldn't have imagined. Nevertheless, we complain about how horrible things are if the economy goes into a slight downturn and a few of us are temporarily unemployed.

Conspicuous consumption isn't something that comes naturally to human beings. The drive for constantly increasing ownership of material goods is a programmed behavior that showed up with capitalism, the Industrial Revolution, and the work ethic. Television also plays a role here. Many of the messages television advertising bombards us with can be detrimental to our well-being. We are led to believe that we will be losers or failures if we don't acquire the latest gadgets and trinkets. We are bombarded with images telling us what sort of people we should be, how we should dress, which gadgets we should own, the type of car we should drive, and the size of house we should live in. Products advertised in commercials promise everything, including self-esteem, happiness, and power. Some of us are made to feel inadequate by these messages because we don't match these images of success. We would all be better off if we didn't see these advertisements.

> To be handed a lot of money is to be handed a glass sword, blade first. Best handle it very carefully, sir, very slowly while you puzzle what it's for.
> —Richard Bach

Underarms that smell like wild roses and automatic climate controls in automobiles certainly aren't the keys to happiness. Consumerism relies on you being constantly discontented. The next purchase is supposed to make you happy, but how could it? You wouldn't purchase anything else if you attained happiness. Consequently, the satisfaction from any purchase is virtually always short-lived and leads to the yearning for something else. Enough is never enough.

How More Money Can Add to Your Problems

Reuters News Service, in April 1995, reported that the bishop of Liverpool called for the government of England to review the concept of lotteries. If nothing else, he suggested that the prizes should be smaller. This was his response after a man in Liverpool committed suicide when he thought that he missed out on a lottery win worth the equivalent of about 13 million U.S. dollars. Timothy O'Brien, a fifty-one-year-old father of two children, shot himself after he failed to renew his weekly bet in a lottery on which he had bet the same numbers for over a year. O'Brien figured he had missed out on the good life after these same numbers were apparently drawn the week he missed placing his bet.

Timothy O'Brien didn't realize that his life may not have changed for the better had he won. Many lottery winners wind up worse off after the big win because of the unexpected problems that accompany having a great deal of money. It is certain the big win wouldn't have brought him happiness, in light of his being the type of individual to commit suicide because of what might have been. It is also almost certain O'Brien would have had many more problems with a big win than without one. Incidentally, at O'Brien's inquest it was discovered that he actually would have won only about one hundred U.S. dollars had he bought a ticket with his regular numbers.

The only thing wealth does for some people is to make them worry about losing it.
—Antoine de Rivarol

Because of the false expectations that we place on being rich, attaining a great deal of money has disoriented many people like Timothy O'Brien. People often say things such as:

> ➤ If I had a lot of money, then I would be happy.
> ➤ If I had a lot of money, then I could enjoy my leisure time.
> ➤ If I had a lot of money, then I would feel good about myself.
> ➤ If I had a lot of money, more people would like me, and then I could find a marriage partner.

If you have any of these thoughts, you are ruled by money and fear. You think that security means having a lot of money. This isn't true. If you believe money is synonymous with security, you won't be happy with the modest amount of money with which many genuinely secure people can be extremely happy. With a modest amount, you will be afraid that you don't have enough to take care of yourself. If you acquire a lot of money, you won't be happy because you will be afraid of losing it. The more money you get, the more afraid you will be of losing it.

An extensive study conducted in 1993 by Ed Diener, a University of Illinois psychologist, confirmed that more money than is needed for basic necessities can't buy happiness or solve problems. In fact, people end up with more problems when they end up with a lot of money. "As you start meeting basic needs, increases in income become less and less important," says Diener. People who receive a pay increase may be happier for a short time, but once they get used to the increase, they set their sights on more and more money so they can fulfill their new expectations. They want bigger houses, fancier cars, and more exotic vacations. These don't provide long-term happiness.

Poor and content is rich and rich enough.
—William Shakespeare

Extra income creates negative effects when people have more money than they need for basic needs and desires. Here are some of them:

➤ Relationships with friends and acquaintances suffer.
➤ Keeping track of one's financial situation becomes more troublesome and time-consuming.
➤ Life in general becomes more complicated.
➤ Fear of theft of property and money becomes more acute as people acquire more money.
➤ Fear of losing money in investments increases.

Wise people tell us that money won't solve all our problems. Many people ignore this wisdom and try to be rich regardless of the required sacrifices. They cling to the belief that money will bring them happiness. In many cases, people also want a lot of money because they think it will bring them power. Of course, people who don't know how to use power end up doing many things that are self-destructive.

Just because 20 percent of us in North America have 80 percent of the money, doesn't mean the rest of you have to be so grumpy about it.

The myth of money is shown to be false by the many people who are wealthy in material goods, but poor in spirit. Although they have a lot of money, they are poverty conscious. They don't know how to spend and enjoy their money. They also don't know how to share their resources with others less fortunate. In North America, the act of giving to the poor is done more by the poor than the rich.

Many people acquire large sums of money through hard work, inheritance, luck, or illegal means. Then they experience disappointment and, sometimes, severe depression. North America has many affluent individuals who have all the material comforts they desire, yet they lead lives of quiet, and sometimes loud, desperation. Experiencing a lingering pain, they understand that there is something missing; there is a big hole that needs to be filled. Regardless of how much exotic food and expensive wine they pour in the hole, and no matter what model of BMW, how big a house, and how much custom-designed furniture they stuff into the hole, the hole gets larger. As the hole gets larger, the pain becomes more unbearable.

Money May Not Be the Best Financial Security

Whether people are working or not working, money is a necessary commodity for their survival. Money is also a means for enhancing the ways in which they enjoy their leisure time. Unfortunately, people look at money as an end, rather than as a means. Looking at money as an end in itself sets people up for great disappointment and dissatisfaction.

Exercise 11-1. How Secure Are You?

Honestly answer these two questions: How much modern-day security do you expect in your life? How much money or how many material possessions do you think are necessary to lead a happy and fulfilling life?

The following letter was sent to me by Lisa Mallet. The last part of the letter relates to money.

Dear Mr. Zelinski

I just finished reading your book *The Joy of Not Working*. It was the most helpful item I've read in a long time. I stumbled on your book by accident. My husband and I were listening to *Cross Country Checkup* on CBC radio. The topic was "Are you working too hard?"

Well, I haven't been working for two years. Your book helped me deal with some of the issues and emotions of being unemployed. I was feeling guilty about quitting my last job. But, looking at the situation now, where I worked was the office from hell that you described in your book. Plus, I was getting migraine headaches twice a week. And over the last two years, this particular company has laid off everyone I worked with. Yet, I was feeling guilty because I quit. And I was worried that I may never find work again.

I don't know what the future will bring, but I certainly have changed my attitude toward work. I'm not sure, just yet, what I will do to generate an income, but I certainly am enjoying my leisure time. And when people want to know what I'm doing, I tell them I'm enjoying the moment, rather than doing nothing. My husband and I are swimming every day, plus I took a pottery class (using a wheel)—it was great fun and I plan on doing more—a great hobby.

The kicker is, I really don't have to work. I am the beneficiary of a trust fund. It doesn't generate a whole lot of income, but it certainly pays the rent and buys the groceries. My husband is retired and collecting a pension. I have always had a fear of not having enough money for retirement. But, if I'm careful, I can certainly make it. Both my husband and I have lowered our cost of living and are living within our means. And it beats working in an awful environment. I have also seen what a lot of money can do to people. There is a lot of money floating around in my family and all of them, except my mother, are very manipulative, back-stabbing people.

Thanks again for the book. It certainly helped me and opened my eyes to a lot of the baggage I was carrying around. Take care.

Sincerely,

Lisa Mallet

Society has conditioned us to believe that we should be preoccupied with accumulating material wealth as security for our retirement and for the unexpected events in our lives. You will have problems with money if you start looking to money for total security. Just as you can't buy love and friends and family, you can't buy true security, despite the things the financial writers in your local newspapers have been telling you.

A million dollars doesn't always bring happiness. A man with ten million dollars is no happier than a man with nine million dollars.

—Unknown Wise Person

Security based on materialistic and monetary pursuits has many limits: The super-rich can be killed in car accidents. Their health can fail just as easily as that of someone with much less money. War can break out and affect the rich as well as the poor. Many rich people worry about losing their money in the event the monetary system collapses.

Total security based on external possessions is another illusion in life. The people who are striving for security are among the most insecure, and the people who least care about security are the most secure. Emotionally insecure people seek to offset their unpleasant feelings by accumulating great amounts of money as security against attacks on their egos. People striving for security by their very nature are very insecure. They depend on something outside themselves, such as money, spouses, houses, cars, and prestige for security. If they lose all the things they have, they lose themselves, because they lose everything on which their identities are based.

It is interesting that the word "security" originally referred to internal—and only internal—security. "Security" is a derivative from the Latin word *securus*, meaning "without care." A truly secure person has an internal security based on an inner creative essence.

If you have your health and the ability to care for yourself, the best security you can have is inner security. Security is the confidence to use your imagination to handle or overcome all the normal problems and situations that confront you as an individual. If you are a secure individual, you have learned how to be "without care." You don't spend much time focusing on financial security. The creative ability to always earn a living is the best

I like money for its intrinsic value, but I always make such a pig of myself with it.

financial security you can have. Your essence is based on who you are internally and not on what you own. If you lose what you own, you still have your center of being; this allows you to carry on the normal process of living.

If Money Makes People Happy, then Why...?

Although most people don't know what, exactly, they want from life, they are absolutely sure that money in large amounts will provide it for them. But most people don't tell the truth about money. Money is more often misused and abused than used intelligently. People make many assumptions about money; most of which are terribly absurd. One assumption people make about money is that money will guarantee their happiness.

Let's put money and its relationship to happiness in proper perspective. Money is an important element for our survival, but how much money we need to be happy is another matter. Hotshot motivational speakers tell seminar participants that millionaires are winners. This implies that the

> When a man says money can do anything, that settles it. He doesn't have any.
> —Ed Howe

rest of us are losers. Quite frankly, I can generate many reasons why most people with very modest means are more likely to be winners in life than many millionaires we have read about in the newspapers lately.

Although money represents power, status, and safety in our society, there is nothing in its inherent nature to make us happy. To give yourself a sense of the inherent nature of money, try doing the following exercise.

Exercise 11-2. Will Money Love You?

Take out the money you have on you or around you at this time. Touch it and feel its warmth. Notice that it is fairly cold. It won't keep you warm at night. Talk to your money and see what happens. It won't respond. And no matter how much you love it, money won't love you in return.

> Plenty of people despise money, but few know how to give it away.
>
> —François, duc de La Rochefoucauld

Money is an expediency in life. To what degree money can enhance our lives depends more on how we intelligently use the money we have, than on how much we accumulate. Michael Phillips, a former bank vice president, thinks there are too many people whose identities are tied to money. In his book *The Seven Laws of Money,* he discusses seven interesting money concepts:

➤ Money creates and maintains its own rules.

➤ Money will appear when you are doing the right thing in your life.

➤ Money is a dream—in fact, it can be a fantasy as deceptive as the Pied Piper.

➤ Money often is a nightmare.

➤ You can never truly give money away as a gift.

➤ You can never truly receive money as a gift.

➤ There are many fascinating worlds without money.

The uses for money are many. No one can challenge the important roles money plays in society and business, but anyone can challenge the myth that a large sum of money is synonymous with happiness. All one has to do is pay attention. Here are just a few significant observations I have made to the question:

If money makes people happy, then…

- ➤ Why did a 1995 study by University of Illinois psychologist Ed Diener show that one third of the wealthiest Americans are actually not as happy as the average American?

- ➤ Why did a recent survey indicate that a higher percentage of the people making over $75,000 a year are dissatisfied with their salaries than are people making less than $75,000 a year?

- ➤ Why didn't Ivan Boesky, who illegally accumulated over $100 million through insider trading on Wall Street, stop his illegal actions after accumulating $2 million or $5 million, but instead continued accumulating more millions until he got caught?

- ➤ Why did members of a family I know (even though their financial net worth is in the top 1 percent for North American families) tell me how much happier they would be if they were to win a major lottery?

- ➤ Why did a group of major lottery winners in New York form a self-help group to deal with post-lottery depression syndrome, a case of serious depression they had never experienced before winning their large sums of money?

- ➤ Why do so many well-paid baseball, football, and hockey players have drug and alcohol problems?

- ➤ Why do doctors, one of the wealthiest groups of professionals, have one of the highest divorce, suicide, and alcoholism rates of all professionals?

- ➤ Why do the poor give more to charities than the rich?

- ➤ Why do so many rich people get in trouble with the law?

- ➤ Why do so many wealthy people go to see psychiatrists and therapists?

The above are just a few warning signs that money doesn't guarantee happiness. As well as anyone, Benjamin Franklin expressed the folly in trying to achieve happiness through money. Franklin observed, "Money never made a man happy yet nor will it. There is nothing in its nature to produce happiness. The more a man has, the more he wants. Instead of its filling a vacuum, it makes one."

Exercise 11-3. Which Is Easier to Come By?

Most people would like to be rich and happy. Which is easier to acquire: a lot of money or happiness? (The answer is at the end of this chapter, on page 192.)

I have a theory about how happy and emotionally "well-off" we will be with substantially more money than we have now. After we have satisfied our basic needs, money will neither make us happy nor unhappy. If we are happy and handle problems well when we are making $25,000 a year, then we will be happy and handle problems well when we have more money. If we are unhappy, neurotic, and don't handle problems well on $25,000 a year, then we can expect the same from ourselves with $1 million a year. We will still be neurotics who are unhappy and can't handle our problems. The difference is we will be neurotics living with a lot more comfort and style.

> Having lots of money doesn't change anything. It just amplifies it. Jerks become bigger jerks, and nice guys become nicer.
>
> —Ben Narasin

Financial Independence on $6000 a Year

You don't have to be filthy rich to sit back and take it easy. As indicated in Chapter 1, the right attitude is important. With the right attitude, you can even live the Life of Riley on borrowed money. By using an idea from Jerry Gillies' book *Moneylove,* you can look at borrowed money as income. If this is too radical for you, because you want to live the Life of Riley on your own money, then you must achieve financial independence. Achieving true financial independence so you can live a leisurely life may be easier than you think. It's not based on high finances.

An important factor for achieving financial independence is first defining financial independence. It may be possible to achieve financial independence without increasing your income or financial assets. All you have to do is change your concept of what financial independence is and what it isn't.

Exercise 11-4. True Financial Independence

Which item from the list below is an essential factor for achieving financial independence?

- ➤ Winning a million-dollar lottery
- ➤ Having a good company pension complemented by a government pension

- Having inherited a bundle from wealthy relatives
- Being married to a rich spouse
- Having hired a financial consultant to help make the right investments

The results from a recent survey indicated that, in order of importance, the biggest concerns for people just before retirement were finance, health, and having a spouse or friends to share retirement. Interestingly, shortly after these people retired, health was considered the top priority and finances moved to third place. Apparently, these people's concept of financial independence changed once they retired, although their expected income remained the same. The results from this survey show that retired people can get by with much less than they first imagine. The survey also supports the notion that no item from the above list is a requirement for financial independence.

Let us all be happy and live within our means, even if we have to borrow to do it.
—Artemus Ward

Joseph Dominguez is financially independent on an income that most people would claim is well below the poverty line. According to Dominguez, true financial independence can be achieved by many more people, if they are willing. True financial independence shouldn't be confused with being a millionaire. Financial independence can be had on $500 a month or less. How? True financial independence is nothing more than having more money come in than goes out. If you are making $500 a month net and spending $499, you are financially independent.

What Dominguez has done for years is live on $500 a month. In 1969, at the age of twenty-nine, he retired as a financially independent person. Before he retired, Dominguez was a stockbroker on Wall Street. He was appalled to see many unhappy people who were living at high socioeconomic levels.

Eventually Dominguez decided he didn't want to work in this environment, so he designed a personal financial program based on a simplified lifestyle. His lifestyle is comfortable, but only costs $6000 a year, which comes from his investments in U.S. Treasury bonds made with money he had saved. Because his needs are so few, he has been able to donate all the extra money he has made since 1980 from his public seminar, *Transforming Your Relationship with Money and Achieving Financial Independence,* to nonprofit organizations.

A Theory to Work or Play With

Dominique LaCasse called me from Vernon, British Columbia, to interview me for a lifestyle article he was writing for *BC Business* magazine. LaCasse and his wife Terri both worked for the *Ottawa Citizen* when they decided to chuck their jobs with a combined salary in excess of $100,000 to move to British Columbia. They weren't sure what they would do or how they would earn a living once they got there. The decision to move was a decision for a change to a saner lifestyle. Here are the first three paragraphs from his article, that appeared in the March 1994 issue of *BC Business* magazine:

> Taking it all in, I find it is more trouble to watch after money than to get it.
> —Michel de Montaigne

Blame it on the margaritas. Or maybe it was all those nights curled up with *The Joy of Not Working,* a seductive but dangerous book by Edmonton-based "non-career planner" Ernie Zelinski. Whatever it was, something had gone to our heads that lunch-hour at Mexicali Rosa's, a restaurant in Ottawa's west end. And our lives were about to take a dramatic and irreversible turn.

It was one of the first sunny days after a long, bitterly cold winter. My wife, Terri, and I, stressed and overworked, had opted for a rare lunch date away from the office in a bid to break the seasonal blahs. Somewhere between the tacos and enchiladas and a pair of fishbowl-sized margaritas, we realized we weren't happy anymore, that we'd stopped following our dreams and that life had become a perpetual work-and-mortgage machine.

By the time the coffee came around, we had decided to quit our lucrative jobs at the *Ottawa Citizen* newspaper and strike out, two school-aged boys in tow, for a simpler, more fulfilling life in Smallville, British Columbia. We were about to become "downshifters," part of a growing number of professionals, business managers, and stressed-out workers who say good-bye to boss and Rolodex and hello to freedom and fresh air. And as we were soon to discover, we would have lots of like-minded company in BC, Canada's de facto mecca for alternative living and a province that owes much of its exceptional population growth to burnt-out Easterners looking for a better way.

Dominique LaCasse and his wife Terri made a drastic change so they would have more control over their lives and the opportunity to live where they wanted. Their decision meant a substantial loss of income and a great deal of uncertainty. However, foregoing extra money, in many cases, leads to a more leisurely and rewarding lifestyle.

The foundations for being happy at leisure are not much different than those for being happy at work. Much of what constitutes happiness has to do with satisfaction. Money has nothing to do with the attainment of satisfaction at either work or leisure. Satisfaction is determined by how motivated we are and how much we achieve at our activities.

> Money doesn't buy happiness, but it pays for the illusion that it does.
> —Unknown Wise Person

Another motivational theory almost as popular as Maslow's theory of the hierarchy of needs is the "two-factor theory" developed by Frederick Herzberg. Like Maslow's theory, Herzberg's two-factor theory has been applied to studying what motivates employees in the workplace. Herzberg never applied his theory to leisure; however, I am going to do it for him because his principles are equally applicable to leisure.

After interviewing many workers in several different industries, Herzberg found that the work characteristics associated with dissatisfaction were quite different from those pertaining to satisfaction. This prompted the notion that there are two significantly different classes of factors affecting motivation and job satisfaction.

As indicated in Figure 11-1, there is a neutral point on the scale where individuals are neither satisfied nor dissatisfied. What will dissatisfy people is the lack of hygiene factors: adequate wages, job security, working conditions, and status. If the hygiene factors are adequately provided, they will not, in themselves, result in employee satisfaction. Only a neutral state—no dissatisfaction—will have been attained.

If people are to have job satisfaction, the motivational factors—recognition, achievement, personal growth,

Of all the ways I have tried to get recognition, this has to be the most creative and the most absurd.

and responsibility—must be provided. These are called motivators because they are concerned with the work itself and, therefore, are effective in creating job satisfaction, which leads to greater performance and productivity.

Let's get back to money. In the workplace, money is important for eliminating dissatisfaction. For an unemployed carpenter who is broke and doesn't have a place to live, money is very important. Getting the money to rent a basic one-bedroom apartment will go a long way to make her life more comfortable. However, once she has enough money to get a basic place to live, getting more money from her job—even enough to buy a 117-room mansion—is not going to do anything towards contributing to more happiness and satisfaction at the job. Her dissatisfaction will have been eliminated, and she will be at the neutral point. Unless she gets some motivators in her job, no matter how much she is paid, she will not attain satisfaction and happiness from her work.

The same principles of Herzberg's theory apply to our leisure time. Money is a hygiene factor that will take care of only so much. Without any motivators in place, the most we can hope for, even with a billion dollars to spend on our leisure, is to get to the neutral state. If we want to create the conditions for satisfaction in our leisure, we must incorporate at least one or two motivators in our activities.

An important ingredient for happiness and satisfaction in life is the opportunity to complete difficult tasks. The more difficult and challenging the task, the more satisfaction we will get from completing the task. For example, one thing people find extremely difficult is to quit smoking. Many people who have quit smoking will say it was the most difficult thing they have ever done. At the same time, they will tell you

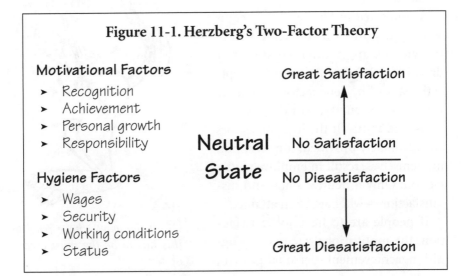

Figure 11-1. Herzberg's Two-Factor Theory

Motivational Factors
- Recognition
- Achievement
- Personal growth
- Responsibility

Hygiene Factors
- Wages
- Security
- Working conditions
- Status

Neutral State

Great Satisfaction

No Satisfaction

No Dissatisfaction

Great Dissatisfaction

that of anything they have done in their lives, giving up smoking gave them the most satisfaction, mainly because it was such a challenging and arduous accomplishment.

A difficult task for me was writing and self-publishing my first book. Self-publishing the book was a great challenge because major publishers told me there was no market for the book. To complicate the situation, I had no experience in publishing and marketing books. I even had to borrow money if I wanted to publish it myself. Nevertheless, I took the risk and published it. The book has been a great success; it is in the top 10 percent in sales of nonfiction books ever sold in North America. Because I was willing to risk and do the difficult and uncomfortable, my life became a lot easier. What I did was incorporate motivators—achievement, responsibility, growth, and recognition—into the activity of publishing my book. I ended up experiencing satisfaction to a great degree from what was a significant personal accomplishment.

If you want to get satisfaction in great measure from your leisure pursuits, ensure you are involved in activities with Herzberg's motivational factors in place. Choosing an inexpensive activity, such as volunteering for a charitable organization, can bring you more happiness than spending $5000 on a new wardrobe. Helping others while working for a charity creates achievement, responsibility, growth, and recognition. The result is a level of satisfaction that no amount of money can ever buy.

Appreciate What You Have and Grow Rich

After his father died in 1971, Jean-Claude (Baby Doc) Duvalier inherited the duty of ruling Haiti. Forced out of office in 1986 by the citizens of Haiti, Baby Doc and his wife Michele weren't content with having stuffed a Air Haiti cargo airplane with a lot of loot. As they were being flown out of Haiti on a U.S. Air Force airplane, they bumped Michele's grandparents, along with nine other passengers, off the airplane, so they could take more loot. Baby Doc and Michele escaped to the French Riviera, where they led the good life, spending millions of dollars a year. Baby Doc and his wife divorced in 1990. While single, Baby Doc squandered all his fortune and was recently evicted from his luxury villa.

When life's problems seem overwhelming, look around and see what other people are coping with. You may consider yourself fortunate.

—Ann Landers

It seems that people like Baby Doc will have money problems regardless of how much money they acquire. Attaining a proper balance isn't the easiest thing in the world. In North America, more money is the common means for acquiring material comfort and achieving social status. Brainwashed that having more material goods means a better life, people gradually and quite willingly end up with financial commitments and responsibilities that are easy to get into and difficult to eliminate. Many people try to maintain a particular lifestyle when they can't afford it. With just a little more prudence in spending, most people can cut their expenses substantially. It is amazing how little people need when they use some resourcefulness.

Jesus, please teach me to appreciate what I have before time forces me to appreciate what I had.
—Susan L. Lenzkes

If you have financial problems, then you must deal with them creatively. As with most problems, financial problems have to be put into proper perspective. For example, if you are in serious debt, collection agents will intimidate you only if you allow them. In North America, you aren't going to be put in jail because you owe a lot of money. When I was living on the poverty line and had a collection agency hounding me for payment of a loan, I had a number of creative tricks up my sleeve to deal with the agent. My ace-in-the-hole solution was to avoid saying anything more once the agent identified himself on the telephone. Instead, I just banged the receiver against the desk until he hung up. It didn't take long for the collection agency to return the account to the lending institution. When I was in a position to pay back the institution, I started making payments on my terms, without having to deal with an obnoxious collection agent.

When one has had to work so hard to get money, why should he impose on himself the hardship of trying to save it?
—Don Herold

Now is the time to pass on the secret of the two powerful ways to handle money, which are equally effective. The first powerful way is to spend less than you earn. If you have tried this and it hasn't worked, the second one is definitely for you. The second powerful way is to earn more than you spend. That's all there is to the money game. Use only one of these powerful principles, and you have handled money successfully.

If you never have enough money, regardless of how much you make, you are probably squandering money on things that you don't need. Finding out why you are a spendthrift living on the edge is important. You must spend some time learning how to handle money. Handling money properly will make you realize that cutting back on your lifestyle and expenses won't make you feel deprived. Try downscaling your spending habits. You will be amazed by how little you actually need.

On the other extreme from squanderers who misspend are the misers who can't spend. They can't enjoy their money regardless of how much they have. If you are one of these people, you are suffering from a disease. You must accept that there is only one reason for having money; the ultimate purpose for money is to spend it. What is the point of having money in abundance if you haven't learned how to spend it? The ability to enjoy your prosperity is essential for fulfillment from what money has to offer. Dream up some creative and fun ways to spend some of your money. If after some time you haven't been able to come up with some good ideas, give me a call. I'll have no problem with helping you spend your money; no amount will be too big for me! I will come up with some fascinating spending ideas that will liberate you from your misery.

After spending some money in his sleep, Hermon the miser was so hopping mad he hanged himself.
—Lucilius

Putting money in its place means that you realize more doesn't mean merrier. Defining your well-being and identity in terms of material possessions and your bank account isn't going to bring you long-term satisfaction. In 1996 Edward Diener, a University of Illinois psychologist, reported that another one of his studies indicated that lottery winners are no happier one year after their good fortune than they were before.

Achieving the goal of making a lot of money won't make you happy. Working hard just for the sake of making a lot of money is an act of desperation. Whether your need is happiness or money, if you chase after it, you are likely to drive it away. As stated in an earlier chapter, once you stop being obsessed with making a lot of money, and instead start doing what you enjoy, you will be rewarded immensely with the satisfaction and enjoyment that you get out of your work. Paradoxically, a great deal of money may also be one of your rewards once you stop being obsessed with money.

Ninety percent of my money I intend to spend on wild women, booze, and good times and the other ten percent I will spend foolishly.
—Tug McGraw

Money should reflect your creative energy and inner security. Using your creative energy while working at a job with a higher purpose will bring the money that you need to lead an abundant life. The more willing you are to risk and follow your inner calling in life, the more money you will attract in the long term. You will also need less money to be happy because your self-fulfillment will come from pursuing your personal mission. Earning a lot of money from your work is just a bonus.

Although you can do without this bonus, you can also celebrate when it does come.

So, put money in its proper place. Discontent may be robbing you of a really good life. You may already have a good life, but you may fail to appreciate it. More money isn't the answer to happiness if your basic needs of food, water, shelter, and clothing are being met. Comparing yourself to others who have more than you will result in discontentment. You will always be able to find someone better off than you. The game of keeping up with the Joneses will result in a game of keeping up with the Smiths, if you ever surpass the Joneses.

Inexpensive Activities Fit for Royalty

Most North Americans have been conditioned to believe leisure is something that only money can provide. Much of what Madison Avenue wants us to do in our spare time is based on conspicuous consumption; it requires that we own a financial gravy train that doesn't lose any locomotion. Creating more spare time is encouraged only for the purpose of buying more "stuff." Excessive emphasis on acquiring money and material things will not bring security. Many things that matter the most don't require much money. In fact, some of the best things in life are free!

A happy heart is better than a full purse.
—Italian Proverb

Leisure goals don't have to be hard on the pocketbook or on the environment. Keep in mind that the most environmentally friendly activities are ones which cost us the least money. Watching sunsets, going for walks, meditating, having interesting conversations, wading through streams, and exercising in the park are activities that cost us virtually nothing and help preserve the environment. These inexpensive activities are also enjoyable enough to be fit for royalty.

Enjoyable leisure is not what advertisers are trying to sell us. Vacations, for example, don't require much money. You don't have to get away to have a getaway vacation. Before venturing across the world in search of greener grass, check out the wonder of the world in your own backyard. Sometimes the grass is greener on our side of the fence. I am not saying you shouldn't see the world. What I am saying is that it isn't necessary to travel to exotic locales to enjoy yourself. Here is another letter relating to money that I received from Dennis Anstett of Calgary.

Dear Sir:

After just reading *The Joy of Not Working*, I felt compelled to drop you a line. Reading—and highlighting—all the common sense was wonderful. Congratulations. The material will help many people get past all the hype that more is better.

My in-laws "retired" in their mid-forties. That was twenty years ago. They were ahead of their time. They now say they have twenty-years seniority in the leisure business. Only government and big business frowns on this mentality. Tough.

I lost my nineteen-year career due to downsizing. It was the worst of times that turned into the best of times. After the transition, which took about a year, my wife and I decided to say good-bye forever to the corporate world. Never again would some entity ever take control of our lives and happiness again.

We just decided we had enough "stuff." And we also had enough of the rat (human) race. We now enjoy a simple, relaxed lifestyle on about $30,000 a year. There is no life like it. For kicks, I wrote a book. What satisfaction! It was never meant to get published. But one thing lead to another. Please find enclosed a sample copy of a self-published best-seller, *The 17% Plan—Investing in Mutual Funds Wisely.*

Although the book is about money and accumulating it, you will notice the philosophy is similar to your own. No one ever said you have to wait until sixty-five to use your RRSP and "retire." My wife and family have been saying for some time that we're not going to be the richest people in the cemetery. We are, however, very rich. We have time—I call it the most expensive commodity of them all. It's comforting to know that many other people feel and think the same way. Mainstream society has got it all wrong.

Sincerely,

Dennis Anstett

In a materialistic world, simple pleasures are easily forgotten. Quality leisure is much more than spending big money on staying in expensive hotels, going on exotic tours, and shopping in exclusive boutiques. In fact, the less we need, the freer we become. Simple lifestyles can become pleasures in themselves. One way to become rich is to pay attention to what we already have. The Buddhists say, "Want what you have and you will always get what you want." Most of us have forgotten about the many riches we have. Many people in Third-World countries would view these as treasures. Books, music, old friends, neglected hobbies, and favorite pastimes are waiting to be rediscovered, if we are willing to overcome our blindness.

That man is the richest whose pleasures are the cheapest.
—*Henry David Thoreau*

Don't base your ability to indulge in leisure pursuits on money alone. More security can come from challenging and refining your beliefs and values than from saving money in great amounts. By developing your interests and hobbies and enhancing the quality in your leisure activities, you will be on your way to having more security than many millionaires. No matter how much money you possess, you can have even greater wealth for enjoying leisure: The wealth is your talent, knowledge, experience, and creative ability.

Answer to Exercise 11-3: Money would appear easier to come by than happiness; this is based on someone's observation that there are no happy neurotics, but there are many rich ones.

CHAPTER 12

The End Has Just Begun

It's Not Over Until It's Over

You may have noticed that this is the last chapter, the end of the book. It may look like the end, but the end has just begun. Yogi Berra made a powerful statement about a baseball game: "It's not over until it's over." This is how you should look at your life, no matter how old you are, or to what age you live. You may be in your early teens or over a hundred years old. Regardless of your age, you should avoid being like many people who are living life as though it was over many years before it's actually over.

> Here is a test to find whether your mission on earth is finished: If you're alive, it isn't.
> —*Richard Bach*

You may have heard the story about the eighty-five-year-old woman who goes to the doctor with an ailment in her right knee. The doctor examines the knee and then states, "Really Mrs. Jones, what do you expect? It is after all an eighty-five-year-old knee."

Not to be swayed by this doctor's preconceived notions about the effects of aging, Mrs. Jones replies, "I beg to differ, Doctor Jensen. The knee may certainly be eighty-five, but this can't be the cause of my problem. My left knee is also an eighty-five-year-old knee, and it's just fine."

All of us, even doctors, can have preconceived notions about how age affects us as we grow older. A Chinese proverb states, "Man fools himself. He prays for a long life and fears old age." Erroneous beliefs about old age can become self-fulfilling prophecies. If we allow ourselves to be influenced by ageism, we will come up with excuses for not pursuing those activities that we can pursue well into our eighties, nineties, and beyond. Old age will be feared if we retreat from life. Taking a new approach to life, rather than retreating from it, is the key to enjoying our later years. No matter what age we are and how close we think we are to the end, we should always look at new opportunities for personal growth, achievement, and satisfaction.

Being over the hill means picking up speed.

The August 1989 issue of the magazine, *The Writer,* reported a ninety-five-year-old former newspaper columnist from Worcester, Massachusetts, Jane Goyer, had just sold her first book for publication to Harper & Row, Publishers. One Harper & Row editor was quoted as saying, "She wasn't signed up because she's ninety-five...but because she's an excellent writer with an unusual perspective who has something new to say." Harper & Row thought this "new" ninety-five-year-old writer showed so much promise that they asked her to agree to an option on her second book. The editor went on to say, "I'm partial to authors who are good investments for the future."

Jane Goyer has shown that youngsters have not cornered the market on accomplishment. Creative and energetic living is not restricted to those with youth and excess energy. Here are a few more examples of people who have lived active lifestyles in their later years:

> ➤ At ninety-four, Bertrand Russell was actively promoting international world peace.

> ➤ Mother Teresa, in her eighties, is as active as she has ever been in helping the poor through her Missionaries of Charity.

- At ninety, Picasso was still active in creating drawings and engravings.
- Linus Pauling, a two-time Nobel laureate for chemistry and peace, was active at ninety, looking for new ways to justify us taking megadoses of vitamins.
- Luella Tyra was ninety-two in 1984, when she competed in five categories at the United States Swimming Nationals in Mission Viejo, California.
- Lloyd Lambert, at eighty-seven, was an active skier and operating a seventy-plus Ski Club that had 3,286 members including a ninety-seven-year-old.
- Maggie Kuhn, in her eighties, was still active in promoting the goals of the Grey Panthers, a seniors group that she helped found when she was sixty-five.
- Buckminster Fuller in his eighties was actively promoting his vision for a new world.
- Harvey Hunter of Edmonton recently celebrated his 104th birthday. (When asked about the secret for a long life, he replied, "Keep breathing.")
- Harvey became a volunteer when he was ninety and started university at ninety-one. He still volunteers one day a week.

These people appear to be somewhat remarkable, and in a way they are. Nevertheless, they are not unusual. Hundreds of thousands of people in their seventies, eighties, and nineties have an incredible zest for life and show great vigor, enthusiasm, and physical ability. To some seniors, being over the hill means picking up speed.

Why Creatively Alive Individuals Don't Need a Second Childhood

After I wrote a magazine article on how people can be creatively alive in their later years, I received several calls from readers. One caller was June Robertson, who was six months away from her ninetieth birthday. The enthusiasm and energy that she expressed on the telephone was overwhelming. I know people in their twenties and thirties who probably haven't shown that much enthusiasm and energy for more than one minute in their lives.

I learned some very interesting things about June. After her husband passed away many years ago, she never married again. Her income has been below the poverty line on occasion, yet she has managed to travel to Russia, Africa, Europe, and India, as well as several other countries. Unfortunately, she had to cancel a visit to China when she became ill, but she still intends to go at a later date.

June became a public speaker in her seventies. She didn't know she could do it until she appeared as a guest on a radio talk show. The people at the radio station liked her so much that they asked her to take over the show for a week. She was paid twenty dollars a day and enjoyed it immensely. She would have done it for nothing. Showing her love for adventure, June went up in a hot air balloon when she was seventy-eight.

When I grow up I want to be a little boy.
—Joseph Heller

All you television junkies, take heed! When I mentioned television to June, she told me that she watches very little TV and called it the "dumb box." Incidentally, she does have an addiction: books. I would say that if anyone is going to have an addiction, this is a rather good one to have.

When I asked June what advice she would give to us on how to live life to the fullest as we get older, she said that first we must not let our spirits down. (Note this relates to attitude, the first thing stressed in this book.) Then she added, "We also must live gloriously, happily, and dangerously."

Seniors like June Robertson, who live life to the fullest, have this enlightened awareness about how alive they really are. They have developed certain character traits that really stand out.

Exercise 12-1. Prime Qualities

Spend two or three minutes thinking about individuals who are in their sixties or older and are still vibrant, active, and enjoying life to the fullest. List the qualities that these people have.

One of the most precious traits that seniors with a zest for life have is their continuing wonder at life, the ability to enjoy each new rainbow, sunset, and full moon. Here are some other qualities that participants in my seminars list for the active and vibrant seniors whom they know:

➤ Creative

➤ Spontaneous

➤ Has a sense of humor

➤ Playful

➤ Energetic

➤ Friendly

➤ Inquisitive

➤ Laughing

➤ Crazy

➤ Able to act foolish

➤ Adventurous

➤ Adaptive

➤ Joyful

> *The only truly happy people are children and the creative minority.*
> —Jean Caldwell

Exercise 12-2. Who Else Qualifies?

What age group other than that of seniors has most or all of the above qualities?

Of course, the other age group with these qualities is that of children. Creatively alive seniors are like children in many ways. They easily adapt to changing circumstances. Being adventurous optimists, they are always willing to take up new activities, such as playing an instrument, public speaking, tennis, or windsurfing. Seniors with a remarkable zest for life make an effort to totally experience each and every single moment. Like young children, they get into the moment fully and become absorbed in it to the exclusion of everything else. Creatively alive adults know how to play, laugh, be spontaneous, and express their joy at being alive. People who are active and happy in their later years don't need a second childhood because they never gave up their first.

> *For the ignorant, old age is as winter; for the learned, it is a harvest.*
> —Jewish Proverb

The Inner World of Leisure

Although maintaining our child-like traits is important for successful aging, our leisure pursuits should go beyond the external world as we grow older. Trying to maintain our youth is not what growing older is all about. Over time, our physical fitness will gradually decline, no matter how much effort we put into being fit. However, our minds can continue to grow and become gradually more fit with time. Continued personal growth contributes to a more fulfilling life because of the increased wisdom and richness we acquire with age.

As you approach or enter your senior years, retirement first enters the picture. Don't ever actually commit yourself to retirement; it should not be taken literally. For those who take retirement literally, death comes much faster because they end up sitting idly around the house. Retirement should be a reorientation of living. We should call the disengagement from a job self-actualization or self-realization, rather than retirement. Either term would signify that we are soaring to new heights, both outwardly and inwardly, in our later years.

Grow old along with me!
The best is yet to be...
—Robert Browning

Again, it is worthwhile to mention Morris M. Schnore's extensive research study at the University of Western Ontario (first mentioned in Chapter 5). Schnore found that a healthy adjustment to retirement was not based on being healthy, wealthy, and highly educated, as previously thought. Although health was important, income and high education were not significant in determining happiness in retirement. Low expectations, positive evaluation of one's situation, self-competence, and internal orientation were found to be the most important contributors to satisfaction in people's retirement.

Commitment to developing an inner orientation is the foundation for an inner world in leisure. Internal orientation may not sound important to individuals in their teens or early twenties, but this is an essential ingredient for self-development as we grow older. This relates to the spiritual self, and is the element in the wheel of life (shown on page 49) that is most neglected, ignored, or denied by people in our materialistically oriented society. The spiritual self is attained through much higher levels of consciousness than those used in sports, entertainment, or working. Communicating with the inner, higher self can be reason enough to live a long life.

Committing yourself to the inner life and the voice within will result in strength and confidence not available in the outer world. Losing contact with the higher self can result in despair and depression in your mature years. The way to escape loneliness and despair is to tune into the spiritual world, which will help you enhance your internal essence. Self-development can be mysterious, but it is also wondrous and fascinating. Self-questioning results in self-determination, which results in great freedom. Realizing your higher self will make you a much more creative and dynamic individual. Your life will be a joy to behold because it has richness and quality.

Walking the Talk Instead of Talking the Walk

Throughout this book I have emphasized many principles for achieving satisfaction in leisure. Here for your review are the most important principles:

- ➤ Ask yourself, How's my attitude today?
- ➤ Don't walk away from negative people: run!
- ➤ Keep focused on your needs and your goals.
- ➤ Ask yourself, "Am I paying attention?"
- ➤ Satisfy three important needs: structure, purpose, and community.
- ➤ Create a leisure tree.
- ➤ Have a balance between active and passive activities.
- ➤ Remember that money will not make you happy or unhappy.
- ➤ Always remember the Easy Rule of Life.
- ➤ Generate many ideas for living.
- ➤ Strive for personal growth, recognition, responsibility, and achievement.
- ➤ If you are bored, remember who is causing it.
- ➤ Don't miss the moment; master it.
- ➤ Remember that the ultimate goal is the process.
- ➤ Be spontaneous.
- ➤ Dare to be different.
- ➤ Risk.
- ➤ Remember that solitude is for secure people.
- ➤ Laugh and be silly.
- ➤ Remember the best things in life are free.
- ➤ Keep physically fit.
- ➤ Take part in eclectic activities.
- ➤ Avoid excessive TV watching.
- ➤ Keep mentally fit.
- ➤ Goof off at times.
- ➤ Develop the inner world of spiritual essence.

> Only a person who can live with himself can enjoy the gift of leisure.
> —Henry Greber

Having developed skills for leisure won't guarantee that you will gain satisfaction from leisure, just as owning a horse won't guarantee you will ride the horse and appreciate it. You have to motivate yourself in some way to do what is necessary to attain satisfaction at anything worth doing.

Many people aren't prepared for a Life of Riley because they don't realize the commitment that is required for getting satisfaction out of leisure. Lynn Bolstad from Toronto wrote to me on January 29, 1993. In her letter below she relates how she was unprepared for a life of leisure.

Dear Ernie,

After reading *The Joy of Not Working* I feel I can call you Ernie.

Congratulations, and thank you for such a wonderful book. I have never believed in "self-help" books but your book is so real and helpful.

Six months ago I accepted an early retirement package (under fifty-five) from the company where I had worked for thirty-seven years. Nothing prepared me for the reactions I experienced after leaving: loss of who I was, fear of the future and a feeling of helplessness after being structured all those years.

So, I decided to give myself some time to sort out what I would do. I spent seven weeks at the beach, just walking, reading and enjoying life. It was the best medicine. I was always involved with not-for-profit organizations through my job. So I am spending more time with these organizations, and I signed up with a seniors organization. Lo and behold, I have been asked to do part-time contract work for a nonprofit group (this is scary but fun).

Your book has helped me tremendously in setting some goals for my new life. I will read it again and again, as I am sure there will be times when my confidence slips. I also plan to give copies of the book to friends as gifts.

Well I'm off to go skating with a friend this afternoon. There is really joy in not working.

Sincerely,

Lynn Bolstad

Lynn Bolstad realized that leisure, like anything else worthwhile pursuing in life, takes commitment. It is one thing to acknowledge problems in life and decide what must be done to change. Most people can reach this point. Where most people fail is in doing something about it. Inaction renders the knowledge of the problem and what to do about it worthless.

There is an old saying: "Talk is cheap because supply exceeds demand." Many people talk about the many wonderful things they are going to do in life, but never get around to doing very many of them. Talking about the walk is one thing; walking the talk is another issue altogether.

Walking the talk is about commitment. Many people use the word commitment, but they don't really know what it means. Using the word because it sounds nice does not represent commitment. The majority say they are committed to being happy and successful in life. Their actions represent the opposite of commitment. When they learn achieving a goal requires time, energy, and sacrifice, they give up the goal.

After all is said and done, more is said than done.

—Unknown Wise Person

Here is a simple test to determine how committed you are to your goals and making your life work: Do you do the things you say you are going to do? This applies to seemingly insignificant items like calling a person when you say you will. If you are not doing the small things, I have a hard time believing you will be committed to larger goals. If commitment is lacking in your life, you won't attain very much satisfaction in the long run.

Your actions are the only things that will attest to your commitment. Your seriousness about commitment will mean you have the intense desire to achieve your goals, no matter what barrier or wall appears in your way. If a wall appears in the way of your goals, you will try to go over or under or through the wall. If this doesn't work, you can go to the left or to the right. If you still aren't successful, you will try blowing up the wall or burning it. Then again, you can always move it.

I'm getting pretty good at this. Maybe I should give other people sleeping lessons.

Leisure provides unlimited opportunities for growth and satisfaction. There is no reason to wind up bored if you are committed to your happiness. So when you find yourself away from the workplace, commit yourself to what has to be done. If after reading this book you still find yourself with too much spare time, then try:

- ➤ Walking to the store rather than driving your car
- ➤ Helping others instead of having others help you
- ➤ Experiencing a sunset for fifteen minutes rather than glancing at it
- ➤ Learning to spend more time alone so you get to experience the pleasures of solitude
- ➤ Reading a good book instead of watching TV
- ➤ Undertaking challenging activities instead of easy ones
- ➤ Finding someone interesting to talk to, someone who is sometimes going to question or disagree with the things you believe in
- ➤ Throwing a party for many interesting people (Don't forget to invite me.)

"As you sow, so shall you reap." In other words, whatever you put in the universe will be reflected back to you. It takes action—plenty of it—to get fulfillment and satisfaction in your life. Don't be like most people, who don't follow through with action. Your positive attitude and enthusiasm for living are the ingredients for being committed to action and a life that works. When it comes to commitment, always remember these words of wisdom from the Buddhists: "To know and not to do is not yet to know."

> There is nothing brilliant nor outstanding in my record, except perhaps this one thing: I do the things that I believe ought to be done.... And when I make up my mind to do a thing, I act.
> —Theodore Roosevelt

Life Begins at Your Leisure

It is my wish that something in this book will help you to spend your spare time with as much enjoyment and fulfillment as I have experienced from writing this book. I trust that the process of enhancing your leisure time has already begun for you; just having read this book is a significant accomplishment in itself.

Now you must do something with what you have learned. Activity and inner mobility will go a long way. You have to love the world to be of service to it. Always try to seek growth, not perfection. You are the creator of the context in which you view things. It is up to you to find a way to enjoy the activities you undertake. Your task is to fill up any idle time, so that anxiety, boredom, and depression have no place in your world of leisure. Let your interests be as wide as possible; the variety in life makes the effort to experience that variety well worthwhile.

When you are feeling no zest for life, find a way to turn on your enthusiasm fast. Routine and the need for security can imprison you to a life of indifference and boredom. Try to deliberately seek new pursuits, just to keep some freshness and excitement flowing. Court the unexpected; invite new people and events into your daily life. Take more chances and risks. Learn to enjoy interesting people, interesting food, interesting places, interesting culture, and interesting books.

I wish I'd drunk more champagne.
—Last words of
John Maynard Keynes

I must also emphasize simplicity. Remember that the greatest pleasures don't necessarily come from spectacular events or incredible moments. Intense pleasure can come from many basic things in life.

You don't really have to seek happiness in your leisure time. Three gifts were given to you when you were born: the gift of love, the gift of laughter, and the gift of life. Use these gifts and happiness will follow you wherever you go.

Keep in mind that attitude is the most important element. By shaping your own attitude, you make life what it is. No one but you gets to make your own bed. No one but you can ever put in the effort to make your life work. No one but you can generate the joy, the enthusiasm, or the motivation to live your life to the fullest.

You only live once. But if you work it right, once is enough.
—Fred Allen

Leisure is a treasure to cherish and cultivate at all stages in your life. If you still haven't realized how precious leisure really is, here is something you should consider: How many people have you heard about who on their death bed said, "I wish I would have worked more." I bet you haven't heard about very many. In all probability, if there is anything you are going to regret not having done in your life, it will be something you could have done in your leisure and not at work. There is a good reason for this: The most precious moments you will experience are those coming from the joy of not working.

Your life begins at your leisure…bon voyage!

Bibliography and Recommended Reading

Anstett, Dennis. *The 17% Plan—Investing in Mutual Funds Wisely.* Anstett Investments Inc.

Bach, Richard. *Illusions: The Adventures of a Reluctant Messiah.* Dell, 1977.

Bolles, Richard. *What Color Is Your Parachute?* Ten Speed Press, 1997.

Bridge, William. *Jobshift: How to Prosper In a Workplace Without Jobs.* Addison-Wesley, 1994.

Dacyczyn, Amy. *The Tightwad Gazette.* Random House, 1993.

Dominguez, Joe and Vicki Robin. *Your Money or Your Life: Transforming Your Relationship with Money and Achieving Financial Independence.* Viking Books, 1992.

Dychtwald, Ken. *Age Wave.* J. P. Tarcher Inc., 1989.

Fassel, Diane. *Working Ourselves to Death: The High Cost of Workaholism and the Rewards of Recovery.* Harper, 1990.

Freudenberger, Dr. Herbert J. and Geraldine Richelson. *Burn Out: How to Beat the High Cost of Success.* Bantam Books, 1980.

Fromm, Erich. *To Have or to Be.* Bantam, 1976.

Gawain, Shakti. *Living in the Light.* Whatever Publishing, 1986.

Gillies, Jerry. *Money-Love.* Warner Books, 1978.

Goldberg, Herb and Robert R. Lewis. *Money Madness.* Signet Books, 1978.

Hanson, Peter. *The Joy Of Stress.* Hanson Stress Management Org., 1985.

Jukes, Jill and Ruthan Rosenberg. *Surviving Your Partner's Job Loss.* National Press Books, 1993.

Kanchier, Carol. *Dare to Change Your Job and Your Life.* JIST Works, Inc., 1996.

Killinger, Barbara. *Workaholics: The Respectable Addicts.* Key Porter, 1991.

LeBlanc, Jerry and Rena Dictor LeBlanc. *Suddenly Rich.* Prentice-Hall, 1978.

Long, Charles. *How to Survive Without a Salary.* Warwick Publishing Group, 1991.

Naisbitt, John and Patricia Aburdene. *Megatrends 2000.* William Morrow & Co., 1990.

Popcorn, Faith. *The Popcorn Report.* Doubleday, 1991.

Rifkin, Jeremy. *The End Of Work.* Tarcher/Putnam, 1995.

Russell, Bertrand. "In Praise of Idleness." In Robert Camber and Carlyle King, eds., *A Book Of Essays.* Gage Educational Publishing, 1963.

Saint Exupéry, Antoine de. *The Little Prince.* Harcourt Brace Jovanovich, Inc., 1943.

Scheaf, Anne Wilson. *When Society Becomes an Addict.* Harper & Row, 1987.

Scheaf, Anne Wilson and Diane Fassel. *The Addictive Organization,* Harper & Row, 1988.

Schnore, Morris M. *Retirement: Bane or Blessing.* Wilfrid Laurier University Press, 1985.

Schor, Juliet B. *The Overworked American.* BasicBooks, 1991.

Storr, Anthony. *Solitude.* HarperCollins, 1994.

Tieger, Paul D. and Barbara Barron-Tieger. *Do What You Are.* Little Brown, 1992.

VandenBroeck, Goldian. *Less Is More: The Art of Voluntary Poverty.* Inner Traditions International, 1991.

von Oech, Roger. *A Whack on the Side of the Head.* Warner Books, 1983.

Wholey, Dennis. *Are You Happy?* Houghton Mifflin Company, 1986.

Resources

Newsletters

Career Planning and Adult Development Newsletter
Career Planning and Adult Development Network
4965 Sierra Rd.
San Jose, CA 95132
Phone 408-559-4946
Contact: Richard L. Knowdell, Editor

The Newsletter of the Society for the Reduction of Human Labor
1610 E. College St.
Iowa City, IA 52245
Contact: Benjamin K. Hunnicutt, Coeditor
$25 per year

ReCareering Newsletter
655 Rockland Rd. (Rt. 176), Suite 7
Lake Bluff, IL 60044
Contact: Sharon B. Schuster, Editor and Publisher

Self-Employment Survival Letter
P.O. Box 2127
Naperville, IL, 60567
Phone 708-717-4188
Contact: Barbara Brabec, Editor and Publisher
Bimonthly; $29 per year; foreign, $33 in U.S. funds

Simple Living
2319 N. 45th St., Box 149
Seattle, WA 98102
Contact: Janet Luhrs, Publisher/Editor

Simple Living News
P.O. Box 1884
Jonesboro, GA 30337-1884
Contact: Edith Flowers Kilgo

Organizations and Support Groups

American Association for Leisure and Recreation
1900 Association Dr.
Reston, VA 22091
Contact: Dr. Christen G. Smith

American Association of Retired Persons (AARP)
601 E St., N.W.
Washington, DC 20049
Contact: Horace B. Deets, Executive Director

Couch Potatoes
P.O. Box 249
Dixon, CA 95620
Contact: Robert Armstrong, Elder #2
TV addict support group

National Workaholics Anonymous
P.O. Box 661501
Los Angeles, CA 90066

North American Network for Shorter Hours of Work (NANSHOW)
P.O. Box 50404
Minneapolis, MN 55405

Overachievers Anonymous
1766 Union St., #C
San Francisco, CA 94123
Contact: Carol Osborn, Founder

Society for the Eradication of Television
P.O. Box 1049
Oakland, CA 94610-0491
Contact: Steve Wagner, Director

Interesting and Offbeat Organizations

Benevolent and Loyal Order of Pessimists
P.O. Box 1945
Iowa City, IA 52244
Contact: Jack Duvall, President

The Boring Institute
P.O. Box 40
Maplewood, NJ 07040
Contact: Alan Caruba, Head and Expert in Boredom

Institute of Totally Useless Skills
20 Richmond St.
Dover, NH 03820
Phone 603-654-5875
Contact: Rick Davis, Master of Uselessness

International Organization of Nerds
P.O. Box 118555
Cincinnati, OH 45211
Contact: Bruce L. Chapman, Supreme Archnerd

National Society for Prevention of Cruelty to Mushrooms
1077 S. Airport Rd., W.
Traverse City, MI 49684
Contact: Brad Brown, President
Slogan: "In front of every silver lining, there is a dark cloud."

About the Author

Ernie Zelinski is a consultant and professional speaker in the field of applying creativity to business and leisure. Uniquely qualified to write *The Joy of Not Working*, Ernie is a connoisseur of leisure who maintains a four- to five-hour work day for four days a week and doesn't like to work at all in any month that doesn't have an "r" in it. Ernie lives in Edmonton, Alberta, Canada, where, besides just hanging around his favorite coffee bars, he enjoys cycling, tennis, reading, and traveling. He is also the author of *The Joy of Not Knowing It All*, a book on how to profit from creativity at work or play.

The author would be pleased to hear from his readers. If you have any questions or comments, please write directly to:

Ernie Zelinski
P.O. Box 4072
Edmonton, Alberta
Canada, T6E 4S8

Ernie Zelinski is available as a keynote speaker and seminar presenter in the areas of creativity and leisure. For more information, please contact: Visions International Presentations, phone (403) 436-1798.

I**f you enjoyed *The Joy of Not Working*, check out these other titles from TEN SPEED PRESS and CELESTIAL ARTS PUBLISHING**

What Color Is Your Parachute?

RICHARD NELSON BOLLES

The best-selling job-hunting book in the world, with over 5 million copies in print, is also full of information and exercises that help the reader to understand just what he or she wants from life as well as from a job or career.
6 × 9 inches, 540 pages, published annually, also available in an audio edition

How to Be Happily Retired

DENIS WAITLEY AND EUDORA SEYFER

An engaging, how-to-be-feisty new approach to living for retired people interested in making the very most of their golden years.
6 × 9 inches, 96 pages, ISBN 0-89087-0

Thinkertoys

MICHAEL MICHALKO

Presents dozens of field-tested, immediately useable tools for generating ideas and stimulating creativity.
7⅜ × 9¼ inches, 352 pages, ISBN 0-89815-408-1

Running a One-Person Business (Revised)

CLAUDE WHITMYER AND SALLI RASBERRY

Tom Peters, author of *In Search of Excellence*, has called this book a "fabulous testament to creating a rewarding lifestyle through your work, whether gardener, physicist, or dressmaker. It's also a no-nonsense, one step at a time primer to getting there from here." Enough said.
7⅜ × 9¼ inches, 224 pages, ISBN 0-89815-598-3

How to Be an Importer and Pay for Your World Travel (Revised)

MARY GREEN AND STANLEY GILLMAR

Completely revised and updated, here is all the information you'll need on where to go, what to buy, how to pay for it, how to get it home and how to sell it.
5½ × 8½ inches, 160 pages, ISBN 0-89815-501-0

To order, or for a free catalog of our over 500 books, posters, and tapes, write to:

Ten Speed Press
P.O. Box 7123
Berkeley, CA 94707

or call (800) 841-BOOK